The Scholarship System

6 Simple Steps on How to Win College Scholarships and Secure Financial Aid

By Jocelyn Paonita Pearson

Trying to figure out how to pay for college without taking on tens of thousands of dollars in student loans? You're not alone.

One of the best strategies to combat student debt is applying to scholarships. The problem is many families get overwhelmed and quit before they even begin!

Join my webinar, 6 Steps to Quickly Securing Scholarships for College, to learn exactly how to help your student avoid decades of debt by securing scholarships to pay the bill - it is possible!

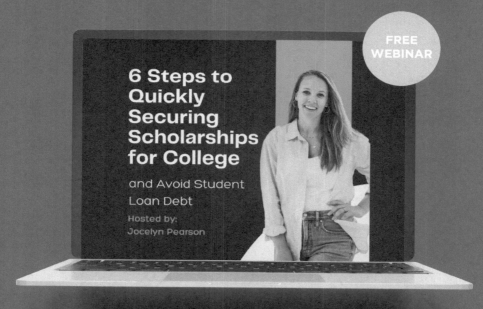

www.thescholarshipsystem.com/freewebinar

Get The Audiobook
and Action Guide FREE!

I've found that readers have the most success with this book when they use the Action Guide as they read. Just to say thanks for buying the book, I'd like to give you the Audiobook & Action Guide **100% FREE!**

www.thescholarshipsystem.com/action-guide

Are you a professional?

Download a free handout for your students and learn about ways to partner with us at
www.thescholarshipsystem.com/partners

CONTENTS

Foreword

It's now common knowledge that the total amount of student loan debt in America has topped $1.76T and the average college student will graduate with around $40,000 in loans. What isn't as well known is the fact that of the $600B worth of loans that are currently in repayment, 1 in 3 loans are beyond 30 days delinquent and 1 in 5 are considered in default (beyond 90 days). The other $600B is held by students either still in school or in forbearance. What we have is the very beginning of a national emergency.

What someone could deduce from these facts is that there is a growing number of students who are finding student loans rather problematic to pay back. Interest rates are higher than they've ever been, tuition has skyrocketed over the past few years, and graduates' chances of being underemployed are just about as good as they are being employed.

Thankfully, there is another way to DO college. The book you now hold in your hands is one of the greatest (and simplest) guides I have ever seen to master the scholarship process. The author is not just a researcher or someone out to make a quick buck by writing a book—she's someone who dominated the scholarship search, application, and collection system to the tune of over $125,000.

I've been delivering a message of financial literacy on college campuses for nearly two decades and have met student after student who received benefit from scholarships. Individually they would tell me they received the Coca-Cola Scholarship, the Gates Millennial Scholarship, lots of smaller awards or a full-ride scholarship from their school. Each had done what was necessary to obtain the award, but none could tell me in exacting detail how they went about the search, application, and interview process... until Jocelyn (Paonita) Pearson.

The process of going after scholarships should be treated like a process or a system, as Jocelyn has so beautifully described in this book. Her notion of "the mindset" is spot on, as is the idea of goal-setting prior to getting started.

If searching for award options is what you dread most, her dead-simple process for searching Google for scholarships is ridiculously good. In short, she's an expert and should be listened to.

What I've found most impressive about Jocelyn and her Scholarship System is the passion with which she wants to share it with the world. She could have been a broke college graduate with tens of thousands in debt, but instead she created a system that afforded her an amazing college experience, zero debt, and a future full of freedom and flexibility. Her goal now is to help others do the same.

Follow her advice, apply the wisdom of this book and the accompanying guide, and take charge of your financial future by graduating with as little debt as possible.

To your future,

Adam Carroll
Chief Education Officer, National Financial Educators
Author, Winning The Money Game
www.AdamSpeaks.com

Introduction

Breaking Down the Barriers to
a Higher Education and Debt-Free Life

Since writing the first edition of The Scholarship System a decade ago, we have reached tens of thousands of families across the country, reviewed thousands of applications every single year, provided tens of thousands of dollars in our own scholarships, and helped students secure well over $13 million in scholarships, a number that is growing every single day.

Unfortunately, while some tactics have evolved with scholarships, the college world and the cost of college has not.

Paying for college is still nearly impossible for most families. It is now said that the average student acquires nearly $37,090 in debt, an increase of nearly 30% since I wrote the first edition of this book; however, the numbers you hear more often are actually anywhere from $50,000 to $80,000 to even $150,000 and higher. When higher education is nearly the same price as a mortgage, and is increasing at a much higher rate than inflation, you have to ask whether the $65,000 salary is worth the price tag. It takes years before you get a return on your investment. Even scarier, it takes an average of 21 years to pay off the student loans (source: Educationdata.org, 2023). This means, if you borrow money for college, you will potentially pay on your student loans longer than you've been alive at this point!

And if you are an average student in the median income level without any crazy circumstances to make you stand out for scholarships, it is especially hard for you. With all these obvious challenges, it is no wonder that students and parents feel discouraged and helpless when it comes to financial aid and paying for higher education.

But I have great news for you—it doesn't have to be such a disheartening situation. You have an alternative option that can not only shockingly reduce the debt you take on (or that your parents pay) but perhaps even boost your spending money while going through college. This option is applying for scholarships and other financial aid. You don't have to pay those crazy prices in order to get a degree, but you do have to go through the steps in order to make it more reasonable.

In fact, the U.S. Department of Education awards an estimated $46 billion and private sources award over **$7.4 billion** in scholarship money annually (source: Educationdata.org, 2023). That is a lot of money out there! Some say as much as $100 million in scholarships go unclaimed each year (source: Scholly, 2020).

You may think that's impossible but we have scholarships email us every single year asking us to send their application out to our members because they haven't received any applications. In fact, I received a scholarship that had a 100% success rate because only four of us applied. They gave all four of us an award! In our earlier days of giving out scholarships, we had a year where we only received 7 applicants for 3 scholarship awards. Those students had nearly a 50/50 chance of winning just by applying.

This truly happens. Scholarships are waiting out there for you. And that is why you're here reading *The Scholarship System*: to help you secure some of this untapped money and avoid being part of a statistic in student loan debt.

Now, this isn't an easy option if you don't know what you are doing. It can be astoundingly overwhelming with dozens of scholarship search engines, thousands of essay topics, and deadlines that range from junior year in high school to senior year in college. There are even scams out there where you fill in your information and it can be sold to other companies. I completely understand how easy it can be to just throw in the towel and give up because you feel overwhelmed or you don't meet the requirements since you are above a certain family income level, do not have a perfect GPA, and you do not see yourself as the next Tom Brady or Caitlin Clark.

There are plenty of reasons why this is a tough thing to do.

That is why I have created this book.

The Scholarship System is going to be your system to make the scholarship process as simple and painless as possible. I will provide you with a step-by-step guide that you can actually implement in fewer hours than a part-time job yet realize the benefits for more than four years later. I've seen many of the books out there and they have some great stuff but the problem is that they are not actionable. You can't read a chapter and get a head start on the scholarship process; you just read about how awesome that person is. With this book, it is the complete opposite. Together, we are setting you up for success, not talking about my own (though I will use other families' stories to teach you)—all you have to do is make sure you are in the money-making mindset and carry through the steps.

I will provide you with simple solutions for applying for scholarships so that you can save time and effort while increasing your rate of return. We will discuss where you can find scholarships that barely anyone else knows about, therefore increasing your chances of winning. We will also boost your chances by covering a fast way to write killer essays that can be perfected and easily reused for other applications. And best of all, I will give you tips and tricks on how you can catch scholarship judges' attention in a good way and make sure your application doesn't get thrown in the trash.

Lastly, I will provide you with over 20 tools and resources so that, by the time you complete reading this book, you will be well on your way to getting your college experience paid for.

These skills that you are about to learn will help you regardless of your ethnicity, gender, income level, or IQ. <u>You can be completely poor or super wealthy and yet you will still be able to implement what we are covering.</u>

As an average student who had to pay for my own degree, I had to deal with the same issues you are facing. I had to figure out where to look and how to apply, what the best essay writing techniques were and how to make myself a competitive candidate. There wasn't a useful guide out there for me to use so I had to struggle to figure out what worked and what didn't. It was extremely painful but I, like you, knew I did not want to be tens of thousands of dollars in debt by the time I was trying to start off my career. What fun is a salary when all of it is going to loan payments?

This is why I am writing *The Scholarship System* for you—so that you can jump right into the scholarship process rather than recreating the wheel and having to go over all the crazy hurdles of applying on your own.

With these same tactics, I managed to bring in $126,400 in financial aid, paying my entire college bill and even giving me some extra cash each semester. I was able to focus on my higher education rather than constantly worrying about money and how much debt I was piling up.

And I am not the only one. We're going to cover dozens of students and families who have managed to do the same with The Scholarship System. We call them #RebelFamilies who said no to the broken college system and discovered a new way to pay for college.

And this is what we are going to do for you together.

I have spent over 14 years learning as much as possible about the scholarship system so that I can equip you with what you need. It is not a long book, so as long as you stay dedicated to the system, you will see the benefits quickly!

With this book, you will have multiple scholarships in the pipeline that actually apply to you. You will be able to win heaps of scholarship money because you will know how to write a killer essay in no time that knocks the judges off their feet. You will also know how to duplicate what we do so that you can keep applying these skills for years to come. Most importantly, you will have money coming your way that will enable you to go to school for a much more affordable price or for absolutely nothing at all!

The Scholarship System is short, sweet, and simple so you can take the lessons out of it and implement them right away.

I promise that if you spend 40 hours a semester following this guide, you will drastically reduce the cost of a higher education, if not get paid to go to school. Now, that may sound like a lot of time but it actually boils down to only 2 hours a week. **Only two hours a week** and you can save yourself years of torture being buried in debt!

Not only that, but if you actually go through all the exercises and resources in this book, you will develop a skill set that also helps you in interviews, class assignments and winning cash awards down the road.

So, before you jump in, I want to give you the single most important piece of advice. Literally, this is the difference between those who get a free ride and those who have to take out loans to eat.

Are you ready?
Here it is....

Do not wait any longer!
START NOW!

I am serious. Starting now gives you the best shot at making college financial aid happen. If you wait and keep putting scholarship applications off, I can't promise you will get anything. The early bird gets the worm, which is insanely true in this case. Sure, you can get scholarships up until your senior year in college, but you still need to START NOW to be debt-free. You don't even have to know which college you are going to in order to begin.

So what are you waiting for? Let's do this!

Start making your way through The Scholarship System so that you can collect your buckets of cash and blast away a future of debt.

Note to Parents:

If you're reading this and you are the parent, guardian or counselor, note that I speak to the student because we want to focus on motivating them. In this updated version, we have added a chapter specifically dedicated to parenting and coaching your student through the scholarship process.

We know the challenge you face in motivating your student, helping them see all they have to offer, and managing this process on top of everything else you have going on. Families are busier than ever yet applying for scholarships is more critical than ever. Student loan debt isn't just impacting students these days—it's impacting the parents and grandparents who are cosigning on tens of thousands of dollars in student debt. An estimated 90% of private student loans are cosigned by a parent, according to the Department of Education, and an estimated 35% regret cosigning on the loans (LendEDU, 2023). 51% of cosigners believe they have to delay retirement due to cosigning (LendEDU, 2023). Overall, the student debt crisis isn't just impacting the current generation but parents and grandparents alike.

This is all the more reason to prioritize this scholarship process. Whether you plan to scrape together any penny you can to help cover the cost, or cut into your retirement (please note—this is a terrible idea. We NEVER suggest doing this), or cosign the student loans, paying for college will have a major impact on you, not just your student.

One mother put it best when she said, "I knew I couldn't pay for college but I could afford a framework that could help my daughter get a free ride." This mother and daughter duo turned that motivation into over $500,000 in scholarships and a completely debt-free undergraduate degree.

But please note: handing your student this book and saying "Figure it out!" may work for some students but it certainly won't work for all. The greatest success stories we have in The Scholarship System made this process a team effort. We'll cover how to do that in our bonus chapter for parents. You can find it after Step 1. For now, I just want to congratulate you on taking the first step toward helping your student pay for college. You are making the decision to become a #RebelFamily where we rebel against the broken system that says students "just have to borrow the money" and instead focus on ways to get a debt-free degree.

And the most important strategy to avoid student loan debt?

Scholarships.

You are in the right place.

Getting in the Money Making Mindset

Have you ever set your mind to accomplish something extraordinary and then realized you just simply never pursued it? I am sure you can think of something you said you would just dominate but never followed through. For me, I have many of these unfortunately. One example would be when I wanted to play softball. After the first season, I never signed up again. I also said I was going to start developing software—that could still happen but, to this day, I just haven't put forth the time and effort to become good at it (or even remotely useful in the subject).

On the other hand, I am sure you can think of many things that you have just stormed through and completely crushed when it came to your goals. Did you say you wanted to get all A's during a semester and then came home with the report card that showed off all your hard work? Did you decide to get a job and save up $1,000? I am sure you were unbelievably proud when you saw your bank account hit four digits. For me, this was my scholarship process. I set my mind to getting my college experience paid for, to have a nice pocket full of money so that I wouldn't be drowning in debt by the end of my four years. By being completely focused on this goal and understanding why I wanted to achieve it, I was able to succeed. I was able to win an astonishing number of scholarships that not only covered my college bill but also gave me money for my expenses.

In upcoming chapters, I will provide you with a scholarship system that is insanely simple if you can stick to it; however, the only way you will carry through and not find yourself disgruntled and ready to quit is if we get you in the right mindset. More specifically, we have to get you in the *money-making mindset*.

So in this chapter, we are going to focus on blasting away any doubts you have about the process and motivate you beyond belief so that you can dominate the scholarship process. Are you ready to make some money and avoid massive amounts of college debt? If so, let's continue.

You can win scholarships, too!

First things first, you have to be confident in yourself and realize that you are entirely capable of winning scholarships. In order to truly believe that you are capable, let's knock out some of the limiting beliefs you may have surrounding your confidence.

Limiting Beliefs

#1: It's too late to apply for scholarships.

Let me start off by saying this is completely untrue unless you are literally about to graduate from college. Yes, that's right. It's not over till it's over. Well, I mean whoever is chosen to sing at college graduation. You can apply for scholarships or even cash awards, which are instantly valuable, as early as elementary school and as late as your senior year in college. Here is a confession: I didn't even start truly applying for legitimate scholarships until my senior year in high school. Now, I don't recommend this because it adds unreasonable stress which you can avoid by starting early, but I say this to show you that it is completely possible to pull off.

Every year in college, I had more and more scholarship money because I didn't just stop applying after high school like most people do. I kept applying and, as I kept applying, I got much better at it. I would knock applications out of the park in no time because I could reuse some of my best essays and I had a fresh start to build my resume when I got to college. But we will get to those tricks later. So repeat after me:

Unless I am about to graduate from COLLEGE, it is not too late to apply for scholarship money or cash awards.

#2: Everyone else is already taking the good scholarships. There is nothing left for me.

I am sure you heard the statistic that billions of dollars in scholarships go unclaimed each year. Having done this for well over a decade, I can personally attest to applications that receive zero applicants. In fact, many reach out to us at The Scholarship System because they need help getting submissions! There is certainly a large amount of money that goes unclaimed each year. Students are so focused on applying for the big scholarships such as the Coca-Cola Scholars Award or the KFC Scholarship Award that they are missing all the little ones with private institutions. In chapter 3, we will show you how to find these little unclaimed monies that certainly pack a punch because they can add up to a free ride. I am going to pick apart stories from multiple students who got free rides this way. But first, I need you to believe that there is plenty of scholarship money out there and it is waiting for one thing: YOU!

#3: I am not a superstar or genius and I don't have any insane stories to share. Why would I get scholarship money?

I wouldn't say I was an underachiever, but I can say that I was no genius with some super IQ and I was certainly no athlete. Even my grandmother will attest to that one after I accidentally threw my bat to third base during my softball game. I think the girl on third base thought I did it on purpose but I honestly was just that terrible. I was an average kid with a minimum wage job at a fast food joint; I had good grades but I didn't really start to focus on them until my senior year in high school and my involvement was mediocre until I got involved my junior year in high school. To top this all off, I hadn't had any horrific experiences in my life, I hadn't survived any life-threatening illnesses and most of my scholarships had nothing to do with my income level at all. Lastly, my SAT score was below average and I didn't even take the ACT.

To summarize, everything I did is absolutely something that you can do too. Super geniuses and future Travis Kelces can get scholarships as well using this system but that does not mean you have to be one! Just realize that <u>there is one thing in life that trumps natural talent</u> and that is **hard work and dedication**. This is a ridiculously important line. In Step 4, I'll show you how to become competitive and increase your chances of winning scholarships, even if you don't think you have anything to showcase. For now, I just need you to commit to the process.

#4: The scholarship process takes too much time.

Applying for scholarships requires time and effort, I won't sugarcoat it. The difference is that it'll take a lot less time and effort because of this book. In your hands, you have a clear step-by-step process to follow to identify, submit, and secure scholarships. Just having this roadmap will save you hundreds of hours and possibly years of frustration.

I can speak from experience. I wasted an entire year applying to scams and not hearing back from any scholarships. I had no idea what I was doing wrong. Once I figured out this system, however, my success rate kept getting better and better. In college, I won nearly every other application I submitted. This also meant the amount of time required became less and less.

In Step 6, we're going to teach you how to take everything you've learned and turn it into a well-oiled system (hence The Scholarship System) so that you can save tons of time throughout this process. We want you to be efficient—and we'll provide you with tips and tools to do so.

Lastly, I want to point out that the amount of time you put into this in relation to the potential payout is astounding. We've had students work

just a couple hours on an application and earn thousands of dollars.
One of our students, Joseph, shared in an interview about his success that he once spent less than 45 minutes on an application and won $600! We'll pick apart his story later but what an amazing hourly rate! He would never be able to get this hourly rate working a part-time job. I always joke I was my highest paid when in college because of this fact!

Repeat after me:

> **I am confident that I can win as much scholarship money as I need. My hard work and dedication is what will win me scholarships. Without this, natural talent can only go so far.**

Reread that sentence quickly.

Excellent. Now that we have blasted away some of your doubts, let's talk about the jaw-dropping power of that hard work and dedication we just mentioned. This is the secret little trick that, honestly, anyone can use but not many people do. It is also the one piece that will differentiate you from most of your peers.

"My son won $76,400 because of what we learned from you! Our income was too high for government grants. We did not have the disposable income to pay for college. We applied to 25 scholarships and he won 13 of them."

– Gay, Mother of Joseph, Who Received Over $76,000

Goal Setting: Your Ticket to Cash

Confidence is crucial to your success but you will build that over time as you start knocking these scholarships right out of the park. One thing you must have in order to get to that point is **hard work and dedication**. There is no way around it. You have to be driven to succeed and truly have a desire for a free ride and debt-free life after graduating. In this section,

"If you don't know where you are going, you'll end up someplace else."

- **Yogi Berra**

we are going to discuss your motivations and goals and how we can use those to keep you at the front of the line in the scholarship process. We're talking about your "why" for doing this.

Let's start off with **why** you even want scholarships or to go to college. You should understand your reasons for doing this process; otherwise, it will be very difficult to make it to the finish line. And no, saying that your mom or your best friend is making you do it is not a good enough reason. If that is truly how you feel, try thinking of why they are making you do this. Dig deep down into your heart and be honest with yourself. It's the only way this will be effective.

Do you want to go to college so you can earn more income and travel? Start your own business? Follow in your parents' footsteps? Become President of the United States? Own a specific car? Save elephants in Africa?

Do you want to earn scholarships because your parents told you to? Or do you want to graduate debt-free and invest your income? Start a retirement plan? Donate? Pursue a master's degree?

These are just a few ideas, but the sky is the limit on this.

Here are directions on how to fill out the chart. This is good stuff so you don't want to miss it. Also, make sure to keep it because you will definitely want these thoughts later on!

1   **My Goal:** We are trying to understand why you would want scholarships, to go to college and to complete The Scholarship System. In the next section, we will let you set up more goals which you will choose, but first we need to think of these three topics.

2   **Why do I want this?** Try to put as many reasons as possible in this box. If you run out of room, that's great! Grab a sheet of notebook paper, copy down the table and keep chugging along. The more reasons you can put in the second column, the better your chances are of winning massive amounts of college financial aid.

3 **Who can help me with this?** This is another area where the more the merrier. Try to think of anyone who has gone to college, won scholarships or can help you go through this book. It can also be someone who perhaps hasn't gone to college but they wish they did and can help keep you motivated to work hard.

4 **What if I do not accomplish this?** Be honest with yourself. How would you feel if you did not go to college? What would be the consequences if you did not get any scholarships? How would that affect you long-term? Sure, people can skip college or just take out loans, but this usually means a greater challenge getting a job or tens, if not hundreds, of thousands of dollars of debt. Once again, try to write as many consequences as you can think of.

My goal	Why do I want this?	Who can help me with this?	What if I do not accomplish this?
Ex: Going to College	To get a great job after graduating so I can support myself	My aunt who attended college, graduated with high honors and got a job	If I didn't go to college, I would not feel accomplished and will have a harder time finding a job
Winning Scholarships			
Going to College			

Whenever the going gets tough, come back to this table and read what you wrote. It will remind you why you are doing all of this and hopefully give you the boost you need to complete the next essay, go volunteer or whatever it is you are having a hard time doing.

It is never fun to do things when you do not understand why you are doing them. When it comes to the scholarship process, you now know why you are doing all of this. The best part is that you also know who you can talk to when it gets really tough. Hopefully you see the value in it. Now, let's have some more fun and let you set up some goals of your own.

Goal Setting Part II

The scholarship process is a major undertaking. There will be times when you feel like you are putting forth tons of effort and not hearing anything back. It's kind of like applying to colleges. For a while, you won't hear anything; next thing you know, you have three different letters in the mail (or your email) all in the same week. Many scholarships are on a similar schedule so this could happen but you can't let yourself become demotivated. You have to hang in there. One way to guarantee that you will keep chugging along is to have little, achievable goals set.

In the table below, set any goal you would like to achieve. It can be about building your resume with activities such as volunteering or getting a part-time job or it can be surrounding the application process, such as how many applications you want to complete in one month or how many quality reference letters you want to have by the end of your junior year in high school. Here are a few more topics that may give you some ideas:

Application timelines	Volunteer hours involvement in organizations	Deadline to have proofreader(s) chosen
Number of essays written before starting college	Run a 10k	Deadline to complete this book
Hike the Appalachian trail		Deadline for completing application research

Tips for Writing Goals

The challenge of goal setting is that many people leave it too vague or they never set an end point. You can see in the table on the next page that I have a task (spending time on scholarship applications), a way to measure my progress (2 hours a week), and I have a timeline which is my light at the end of the tunnel (when I graduate high school). Now, unless all the scholarships you receive renew each year, I would suggest doing this during your four years in college so that you can make sure you continue to have enough, but let's leave it like this for now.

When you write your goals, try to structure them like the example. Here are the three characteristics of a great goal:

- It is specific and realistic.
- It is measurable.
- It has a timeline.

Another key to a successful goal, believe it or not, is telling people about it. This is helpful because they then hold you accountable. Every year I attend a conference and come back with a ton of goals. If I kept them to myself, I would easily be able to let one drop to the side. However, because I tell multiple people my goals and sometimes even ask someone to be my 'accountability partner,' I feel a greater urge to actually carry through with them.

We are going to do the same for you.

In the table, write your goal and why you want to achieve that goal, as well as select someone who will not only hold you accountable to make sure you are actually completing your goals, but also help you when you get stuck. Like I said earlier, there will be times when you want to quit. That is when these accountability partners are like gold. They push you and motivate you to keep going.

Last tip before letting you set your goals: create reminders. This can be a marker board with your goals written on them, or a reminder in your phone or calendar. You can even print this sheet out and tape it on your bathroom mirror. Just use something you know you will look at frequently so that you are constantly challenged to finish what you set out to do.

Okay, now it is time to set your goals. Have fun with it! If you run out of room, feel free to grab a sheet of notebook paper, copy down the chart and continue. Just make sure you are being realistic and try not to overwhelm yourself.

My goal	Why do I want this?	If I get stuck?
Ex. Spend an average of 2 hours/week on scholarship applications until I graduate high school	So that I can get a free ride to college and not be bogged down by debt when I graduate	My mother – she can keep track of my efforts, push me to stick to it and reward me when I do

The main reason we are setting all these goals is to help you stay dedicated to this process and maintain that desire for a free ride to school. They wouldn't send soldiers out on a mission without setting goals first; that would be a complete failure. This is the same scenario. You cannot complete the scholarship mission without having clear goals to keep you directed and motivated.

We have 2 more topics to cover and then you will hear from another student who got her entire college experience covered by scholarships. You don't want to miss this one because she gives you some of the challenges she faced as well as her major piece of advice in order to be successful in your scholarship search.

Let's quickly talk about how the people you choose in your goal charts can hold you accountable and how you can hold yourself accountable. You may think knowing that you will have a nice pay check at the end of this process is enough, but, believe me, the light at the end of the tunnel can seem pretty far away at times. This is where these tactics come into play.

You have already decided the who; now let's discuss the how. How can your accountability partner or accountability 'buddy' make sure you carry out these goals?

I would suggest setting up weekly or bi-monthly meetings. These can be very short if you are both busy, but just a way to check in and see how you are doing. You can meet over the phone, via Zoom or Facetime, or you can do it in person. The method isn't as important as you just talking about your status on these goals; otherwise, you will start shuffling your feet and slowly slip on the goals.

Now how can you hold yourself accountable?

We already talked about setting reminders and having your goals in a place where you can constantly see them such as on a marker board or your bathroom mirror. One more tip is to start a Google Doc or Word document (I like Google Docs because then you can also share this with your accountability buddy) and take just 3-5 minutes a day to write the following items:

- What is the date today?
- How many hours did you work on the scholarship process? (This can include volunteering, extracurricular activities, anything you do that helps make you more competitive but you need 2 hours a week on actual applications/essays.)

- What did you accomplish? (Not what you did; what did you actually accomplish?)
- What problems did you encounter?
- Do you need anything from anyone?

This should **never** take you more than 5 minutes. If it does, try limiting your responses to 5 words maximum per question. You should just add each day below the other and slowly grow the document.

The greatest thing about this is that you can then go back when you are receiving all that hard-earned scholarship cash and actually see the progress you made. This slowly becomes a journal of all your challenges and triumphs so you will feel <u>amazing</u> after reading the document.

Let's discuss what we covered.

First, the key to surviving the scholarship process is having the right mindset. Specifically, it is about having the money-making mindset. In order to have this mindset, we first blasted away your doubts about the scholarship process and helped you realize that you are completely capable of getting scholarship money. Natural talent is great, so if you have that, it will certainly come in handy as we go on. However, what really matters is your willingness to push through this process and put forth the effort to win the big bucks. Hard work and dedication trumps natural talent any day. If you have both, you are a lethal weapon. But if you don't think you are a super genius or anything like that, do not worry. Your efforts are what matters.

You then set some goals. First, you wrote down your motivations for why you want scholarships and why you want to go to college. You then got to create some of your goals. The cherry on top is the person you chose to hold you to these goals. Having someone to push and motivate you when times get tough is extremely important. Even more important is your ability to hold yourself accountable. We covered some basic tactics that will help you do this.

I have faith in you. You can do this. No one wants to leave college in massive amounts of debt. That not only takes away from your salary you have been so excited about, but it also destroys your opportunities in college and out. Don't let debt shatter your future—get in the money-making mindset and let's get you some scholarship money.

In the next chapter, we will explain how to navigate the crazy scholarship system. You cannot begin if you do not understand what exactly you should be applying for. Chapter 2 will be focused on giving you an understandable breakdown of college financial aid. Before we get there, here is some advice from Jenn Frazee, a college student who managed to get paid to go to school.

What was your greatest challenge finding scholarships?
My greatest challenge in finding scholarships was finding ones that applied to me. There are many, many scholarships out there for high school students, but many of them have extremely specific criteria. Local (as opposed to national) scholarships give you the best odds of actually receiving them (due to fewer applicants/competition), however many of them require your parents to be a member of a certain organization, you to be of a specific heritage, or for you to have a specific intended major for college. The biggest stipulation is usually financial need, and many students believe that they do not qualify for this specific type of scholarship. If it is required that you receive federal aid or something similar, and you do not, this obviously disqualifies you, however if the 'proof of financial need' is less specific, you should always apply anyways, because you never know what the specific organization will consider. Despite all these restrictions, I was still able to apply for about 50 different scholarships, local, national, and school-specific.

If you could give one piece of advice to students who are looking for scholarships, what would it be?
Be persistent! It is easy to get discouraged and bogged down in research and applications; however there are tons of scholarships out there that never even get given out, because no one applies! Even if you only receive 1 out of 20 scholarships that you have applied for, it will be worth the work when you save thousands

of dollars on your education. Start early, create a strategy, and apply for as many scholarships as you can! Overall, just don't give up, because that's what the majority of students do, and if you can stick it out through all the hard work, you will be rewarded.

Guiding Your Student Through The Scholarship System

If you are a parent, guardian, counselor, or some other mentor hoping to help a student through the scholarship process, this chapter is for you! Over the last ten years, I've seen where families get stuck in the process. There is no shortage of parents who tell me, frustratedly, "I can't get my student to do this!" That is why, in this new edition, I wanted to create a chapter to share the strategies we've learned to make this a productive process, rather than one that ages you.

It is no secret that this process requires work. If it didn't, everyone would have a free ride. However, with The Scholarship System, it will require much less work than if you were to figure this out on your own or have your student figure it out. Still, it does require dedication and effort. For many of the most successful families we've worked with, success happened when it became a partnership. That is why I am so excited you are here reading this right now. You are clearly invested in your student's success with scholarships. I am going to share a few ways you can help improve their chances, but before I go there, I want to share some things you absolutely should NOT do.

How NOT to Help Your Student Through the Scholarship Process

First, do not do the applications for your child or student. Committees know better. I've had the honor of interviewing scholarship committee members that have awarded millions of dollars before, and this was one of their main grievances. It is very clear when a parent writes the essay or does the application. Additionally, you are not only adding work to your own plate, but you are robbing your child of a huge opportunity to learn critical skills for long-term success in college and beyond. We've all heard of helicopter parents yet none of us want to be one. In this case, you must fight the urge to do the applications for them. Yes, it'll take more time to coach them and review their materials, but think of it as an investment in their future because that is exactly what it is. Helping them figure out how to sell themselves, write about themselves, gather thoughts and communicate them professionally, and all the other skills they will learn will help them in the scholarship process, admissions, job search, interviews, the business world, and so much more. I'll never forget when one father emailed me only a week into being a course member saying, "I am blown away. Even if my daughter doesn't win a scholarship, I can already see how many life skills she's learning by going through your course." Your student can too.

Second, do not handle the communication on their behalf. One exception may be regarding FAFSA results and communicating with the financial aid office since they often need your financial information, but otherwise, let your student do the emailing and calling. Again, this is a critical life skill but more importantly, it leaves an impression on the scholarship committee when they are responsible enough to do so—and leaves a negative one when they aren't. In another interview with a committee member, she remembered a student who replied to an email with "Ya." She was blown away and couldn't get it out of her mind when they were going through applications. Alternatively, students who write professional, mature emails will leave a positive impression.

Lastly, don't leave the process entirely up to them. Even if you must work on your own tasks, pay bills, email your colleagues or whatever you need to do, doing so while they work on scholarship applications will be extremely helpful. More on ways you can support them in a bit, but leaving the entire process up to a teen often leads to frustration, overwhelm, and little results. Now, fortunately, with The Scholarship System, they have much more guidance than they would without it. Still, there are little ways you can drastically increase their chances of success, which means fewer student loans for them, and possibly less cosigning on student loans for you!

Now that we've gone over a few things not to do, let's discuss what to do.

How to Help Your Student Through the Scholarship Process

Scholarship Sundays

One of the strategies we teach in The Scholarship System course is something I call "Scholarship Sundays." It doesn't necessarily have to be Sunday though. You and your student can pick any day of the week that is consistently open or flexible, along with a specific time—I recommend 1-2 hours—and sit down to work on the scholarship process. This is also a great time to work on admissions if you're in the thick of things with that. The goal is to have a dedicated meet-up time each week to work on the college process.

Our families that have implemented Scholarship Sundays have seen major success. Why? Because it alleviates the other six days of the week from having to nag them into working on scholarships. It takes you out of that parenting and oversight role during those days and gives BOTH of you a break for a bit. It also sets a clear expectation. That meeting time is not up for debate. They know it's coming and so do you.

What can you do during this time? You and your student can choose if you want it to be a working meeting where they are actually knocking out applications (Step 5) or if it should be more of a check and review where they bring completed materials and you spend the time reviewing them together. This will also vary based on your student and how disciplined or busy they are through the week. While your student is working on an application, you could continue building their list of scholarships (Step 3). This brings me to my next suggestion on how you can help your student through this process. But first, a few comments from other parents on Scholarship Sundays:

"So we ran ours a little different. It was more like a meeting. She would show up with her essays done from the previous week. We would get what was needed for each packet to be sent out. That was the first hour. 2nd hour we would then research and find 3-6 more that she was eligible for. See what needed to be tweaked in core 4 essays and wrote a checklist for each set. She would do the work during the week, we would finalize on Sunday, I would mail stuff out for her on Mondays."

– Meredith, Parent & Course Member

"We implemented a 'Scholarship Sunday' at our house once a month and spent a few hours working on scholarships and reviewing the ones with upcoming due dates. We made it fun and always had snacks and something fun to do when we completed all our tasks. These Sundays also gave us time to talk about many topics that were important to us with her leaving soon for college. In the end, she won over $15,000 in scholarships for her freshman year of college and, after being selected as a Resident Assistant in her sophomore year, we found out that the university she attends actually owed her money for that year of school (we got a $1,000 refund check EACH semester!). Since then, we've tried the same strategies with our second daughter. She has now secured $9,125 in external scholarships (not including the scholarship money she has received from her university). In the end, what made them successful was persistence, dedication, and good old-fashioned teamwork."

– Tracy, Parent & Course Member

And lastly, just to give you a little laugh and know you're not in this alone:

"Scholarship Sunday a little rough today."

- Nina, Parent & Course Member

Building a List of Scholarships

If you want a more visual training, I have a free webinar for parents on how to find legitimate, less competitive scholarships your student can actually win. You can go to **www.thescholarshipsystem.com/freewebinar** for the free training.

Ultimately, helping your student build their scholarship list is a great way to share the workload without crossing boundaries on letting them do the bulk of the work. Also, you will most likely be better at discerning whether a scholarship is legitimate or not. For tips on how to build a scholarship list, identify if it is a scam or not, and more, be sure to read Step 3 in this book.

Additionally, there is a bonus chapter on documenting scholarships right after it. I highly recommend you and your student use our Chrome Extension and mobile app to save scholarships. You can share the same login and, if you have multiple students, label which scholarship is for whom. No matter which method is best for you and your student, helping them set up a system in general will also help increase their chances of winning scholarship dollars.

Brainstorming Activities, Awards, and Strengths for Scholarship Apps

For many students, selling themselves can be a challenge. In Step 4, we discuss how to discover competitive factors as well as create new competencies. Sometimes, however, they need some help to see all their amazing accomplishments. This is where you can come in. Helping your student brainstorm what they've done in the past that could be used in essays and applications may uncover things they either forgot about or totally discredited. If you are a course member, we have an activities sheet for students to fill in or you can make your own. Updating this together every single semester can make life much easier down the road!

Reviewing Essays and Applications

Every single submission and revision needs a second (or third) set of eyes. For some, parents or guardians can fulfill this role. For others, they may go to an English teacher or professor or some other qualified professional. If you decide to handle this role, please make sure you are truly comfortable and qualified to do so. Scholarship essays require a specific type of writing. They aren't like a term paper but need to be creative, thought-provoking, and engaging. We cover our 3-step writing method in Step 5. That said, not everyone is cut out for this kind of writing (or editing).

I always joke about a time my father helped review my sister's math homework. When it came back reviewed, we could see some correct answers were erased and replaced with incorrect ones. Guess which ones my father suggested were incorrect? The correct ones! We always tease him about math not being his strong suit (he has many other strengths, of course). But let's just say we never asked him for help on math homework again. If English and creative writing are not your strong suit, it's okay to take a back seat on this one.

"Something helpful I started doing for my son. We have a shared Google Doc that I go through the app and list each scholarship due in that month and what is needed to complete that scholarship. As we get the information needed or he gets the essays completed, I strike-through those items. We can instantly see what is needed, and it puts a visual in one place for my son. He stopped feeling overwhelmed once I did this. Before, I would tell him he's got 10 scholarships to apply to this month and it just seemed overwhelming to him. But doing this, especially when I highlight the essays he's already completed, he can see it's not that much work. I am attaching a photo. It's not pretty, but it gets the job done."

– Audra, Parent & Course Member

Motivating Your Student to Apply for Scholarships

Now let's say you are ready to go on this process and eager to help, however, your student keeps avoiding the process or dragging their feet. This is common! They are teens and young adults, after all. You may be lucky and have a self-starter or your student may need a little extra support. For this, we brought in a teen psychologist and expert, Dr. Maggie Wray, to speak to our course members. We narrowed it down to two different approaches. First, find out what is holding them back. Second, find out what will motivate them.

What Is Holding Your Student Back

Many parents assume their child or student is being lazy when it comes to scholarships; however, we've found that it may not always be the case. Many times, students are self-conscious or think they would never win so why bother applying. Talking them through those limiting beliefs may help them overcome the procrastination. You can point out all the wonderful things they've accomplished or show how passionate they are in one area or another.

Another reason some students aren't applying is because of overwhelm. In that case, we want to assign them just ONE step in The Scholarship System and have them start there. Perhaps we just want them to find 3 scholarships they can apply for. Or maybe you find one and they just need to write one essay. If you're a course member, we have a "quick-start scholarship assignment" under Start Here just to give them a taste and build momentum. Breaking the process down into bite-sized, approachable pieces will help them take steps forward. This is what The Scholarship System is all about!

Ultimately, we may have to boost their confidence or help them choose the first step to get them to get going!

What Motivates Your Student

After ensuring there aren't any limiting beliefs in the way, we next need to figure out what will motivate our student. For some, numbers talk. For others, they need a more reality-focused or creative approach.

Here are some of the suggestions we brainstormed:

* Walk your student through a calculation to see what the alternative is, meaning their student loan payment if they were to borrow the money. For your numbers-driven students, this may be enough. That figure alone may scare them into wanting to avoid it! For others, we may need to get creative. Regardless, it is helpful to have them dream up what they could use that money for instead. Student loan payment will be $600/month? What do they love? Travel? Entrepreneurship? Nice cars? What would that $600 equate to if it didn't have to go toward a student loan payment?

 COURSE MEMBERS

You have access to our College Cost Calculator to help compare the costs of colleges and calculate student loan payments under Step 2.

- Calculate an hourly rate based on spending just a few hours on a scholarship application and compare it to how many hours they would need to work in order to earn the same amount; e.g., if they spend 4 hours on a $500 scholarship and win it, they made $125 an hour and most likely now have a reusable essay. If they're currently making $15/hour at their part-time job, they would need to work at least 33 hours, not including time to cover taxes. For some students, especially those who work, this approach may help!

- Lastly, there may need to be some tough love. Some students don't realistically think through how they are going to cover college. As a parent or guardian, if they plan to borrow over the maximum amounts allowed through government loans, you will be responsible for cosigning those loans. This means you are 100% on the hook for them if your student doesn't pay them back. Some parents don't want to commit to that (or can't!), which means their student either has to find a more affordable school or secure scholarships to bring down the cost. No matter what, this discussion is critical to help your student understand the importance of applying for scholarships.

In the end, there are many ways to get involved in the scholarship process but ultimately, we want it to be a team effort. I know you'd love to have your student take this book and run with it. For some, they may! But others may need more support. In that case, I hope this new bonus chapter gives you some helpful ideas.

If you want to attend a free webinar all about the scholarship process and see what other parents and guardians are doing to help their students, go to **www.thescholarshipsystem.com/freewebinar**.

Understanding College Financial Aid 101

Reading about scholarships and other forms of aid can be dreadful. You hear words and acronyms like grants, FAFSA, merit-based, EFC (SAI), and many others that may not make sense. It can be so overwhelming! In this chapter, I am going to explain all of these to you so that you can start the process armed with one of your greatest tools—knowledge. I once met a student who accidentally borrowed $13,000 thinking it was debt-free financial aid. This is why it is so important to understand the difference between these terms.

To make it more interesting, we are going to choose a college, write down how much it costs, and then run through the true cost depending on which forms of aid you use.

 COURSE MEMBERS

If you are a member of *The Scholarship System* online course, we have a great tool, our College Cost Calculator, that will walk you through and do the calculations for you! You can even compare multiple schools and add in scholarships to understand your true cost of college.

Let's first calculate how much your college experience will cost per year. If you do not know your college yet, just decide private or public school? In-state or out-of-state? Then you can take the average costs from the College Board's site. Or you can just pick one of the schools you are considering and find their figures on their financial aid website. Now I don't want to scare you, but you must include at least a 2-4% tuition increase for each year until you actually go to college. To calculate the increase in tuition, fill out the formula below:

(Annual Tuition Amount x (1.025)^years until college)

Waiting three years until school with out-of-state tuition in this sample would be: (28,461 x (1.025)3) = $30,649.38

You can also use this equation: (28,461 x 1.025 x 1.025 x 1.025)
Put the number you calculated in the tuition line below. If you go to college next year, leave the tuition amount as you originally found.

Next, fill out the form on the next page. When calculating these expenses, assume only 9 months for when you are in school, which means summer expenses have to be covered by a summertime job or some income source other than debt or scholarships.

For example, if you spend $40 per month on gas, type in $40 x 9 = $360.

Keep in mind, however, that if you make applying for scholarships your 'job' in high school, you can get paid to go to school and perhaps even have some leftover funds to help in the summer.

Also, there are ways to make these costs lower, such as leaving your car home your freshman year like I did. That's another discussion for another day! But know the less you have to pay, the easier it will be to get to that free ride.

College Cost Calculator

Annual Figures	Sample University	Your University
Wages	$3,600.00	
Gifts	$0.00	
Allowance	$0.00	
Financial aid	$0.00	
TOTAL Income	$3,600.00	
Tuition	$30,649.38	
Fees	$900.00	
Books	$1,000.00	
Supplies	$400.00	
Traditional Dorm Housing	$5,988.00	
Car Insurance	$720.00	
Gas	$360.00	
Car Maintenance/Repairs	$200.00	
Parking	$560.00	
Cell Phone Monthly Plan	$45.00	
Entertainment	$722.00	
Personal Expenses	$350.00	
Food/Household Expenses	$3,021.00	
Gifts	$0.00	
Medical Expenses	$130.00	
TOTAL Expenses	$45,045.38	
(Expenses - Income)	**$41,445.38**	

Definition 1: FAFSA - Free Application for Federal Student Aid

Many families do not fill this critical form out because they believe their income level is too high. I have one of the biggest pieces of advice regarding the FAFSA right here: **APPLY!**

Many schools won't even consider you for their own funding (regardless of your chances of getting federal aid from the government) without this form. In fact, one family had a coworker tell them not to bother applying so they didn't. By the end of their daughter's freshman year in college, they were struggling to pay the bill and met with the financial aid office. The office had them complete FAFSA and discovered that had she submitted the form her senior year in high school, she would have received over $17,000 a year from the school. The worst part? That type of aid is only awarded upon admission, so she was no longer eligible to have it added to her financial aid package as an enrolled freshman! **The family missed out on $68,000 in aid from the college.**

One more quick story—one student was applying to NYU and didn't realize they had their own specific deadline to submit FAFSA (earlier than the FAFSA.gov deadline) and therefore missed it. This student found out he missed out on $40,000/year!

In the end, hopefully you now see how important submitting FAFSA can be. If your parents make six figures, you may not get any income-based funding, but you can still get unsubsidized or subsidized loans. I will explain what that means in just a minute, but just know that subsidized loans versus one through a bank or private institution can save you tens of thousands of dollars. Additionally, FAFSA may be required to be considered for non-need-based aid at your university. **No matter how much money your parents or guardians make, you should fill out the FAFSA.**

You can find details on how to apply at www.fafsa.gov, but here are some key things to know about the FAFSA:

1 Apply as soon as you can. <u>Some FAFSA awards and loans are given out on a first-come, first-served basis.</u>

2 You must apply **each year.** The good thing is that, if you have siblings, your parents only have to do it once per year for each of you.

3 FAFSA awards can either be grants or loans, but your Student Aid Index, (SAI), previously known as the Estimated Family Contribution, (EFC), which is calculated by FAFSA, can also help you get scholarships with your university and other private companies.

4 Most people do not know this, but if you do not receive the maximum amount of grant money through FAFSA, you can call your university's financial aid office and <u>ask them to reconsider</u>. Ultimately, the school has power over the amount within the limit. They can increase your grant if you are truly in a financial bind.

This is called a financial aid appeal. Many schools have a specific process in place to request additional aid. Just know you will need some sort of extenuating circumstance such as excessive medical bills, loss of a breadwinner, loss of a job, or something else that drastically changed your financial situation from the one depicted on the FAFSA form.

For sources of funding, let's start off with the worst-case scenario: you have to borrow all funding in order to go to college. The good news is that **85% of students receive some sort of financial aid** so do not let this section scare you. It should motivate you, however, to NOT want to deal with interest. Here we go.

Definition 2: Loans

Loans are debt which will be paid back at a higher amount than you borrowed. They can be split into three categories: subsidized loans, unsubsidized loans, and private loans.

Subsidized loans are much better than unsubsidized. When I mentioned earlier that applying for the FAFSA is valuable even if you are at a higher income level, it is because of subsidized loans. According to savingforcollege.com, for students with parents who earn six-figure salaries, nearly a third (32.9%) of students received institutional grants, over a fifth (21.4%) received merit grants, and more than a tenth (11.6%) received need-based grants. Yes, we would like these percentages to be higher but the point is this: please apply for the FAFSA!

If we have to borrow money, which type is better? Subsidized loans. Why? Because they do not accumulate interest while you are in college. The current maximum is about $19,000 for a four-year degree, which would accumulate around $2,000 of interest while in college. However, with subsidized loans, you do not build up that extra $2,000. Instead, when you graduate, you still only owe the $19,000 you borrowed. Then, like other loans, the interest begins to accumulate once you graduate.

Alternatively, unsubsidized and private student loans accumulate interest from the minute you borrow the money. This means, when you graduate, the $19,000 you borrowed would actually now be nearly $21,000 and the new interest will be calculated on this total, not the original $19,000. Unfair, I know. But at the very least, maximizing subsidized loans can save you a few thousand dollars!

One limitation with government loans that you need to keep in mind is that there are indeed limits each year. For example, for the 2024-2025 school year, the subsidized limits are $5,500 for a freshman, $6,500 for a sophomore, and $7,500 for a junior or senior in college. Then you can receive an additional $2,000 per year in unsubsidized loans.

This is important to keep in mind because these are most likely the only loans you'll be able to borrow on your own without a cosigner, yet they are limited to about $30,000 over 4 years. That means if you need more than that, you and your parent or guardian will have to apply for either Parent PLUS loans or private loans, which will require a cosigner. You cannot just borrow $168,000 on your own (for good reason!).

*If you have to borrow private loans or simply want to read up more on student loans, interest, and how it all works, you can check out our blog post on "How Student Loans Work" at **www.thescholarshipsystem.com/ lenders**. My goal is that you won't need this, but I also want to make sure you're an educated borrower if you do! Also, keep in mind that you could continue applying all throughout college, so don't think if you had to borrow for the first year, you will have to for the remaining years. That can change if you implement this system!*

Now it is your turn. I won't ask you to deal with calculating this on your own because there are some great calculators online that you can use. Just Google search "student loan calculator" and be sure whichever one you choose allows you to select "pay/accumulate interest while in college" because this makes a difference. I tend to like calculator.net.

 COURSE MEMBERS

For those who are members in The Scholarship System online course, you can just fill in the College Cost Calculator under Step 2 and it'll automatically do the loan calculation for you!

1) How much will four years at your college cost you if you have subsidized loans (remember: only up to the limits above per year)?

2) What will your monthly payment be after graduation?

3) How much will four years at your college cost you if you have an unsubsidized loan (remember: only up to the limits above per year)?

4) What will your monthly payment be after graduation?

5) Run the same calculation for the amount you totaled in the previous chart where you budgeted for an entire school year. Remember those costs are only for one year so you need to calculate the total borrowed if for all four years.

You will find that if you borrowed over $150,000 like in the sample, your payments will be nearly $2,000/month after graduating!! Based on average salaries, most graduates cannot afford that kind of student loan payment.

Maybe you find these amounts are less than you expected. Either way, $150,000 or more is a lot of money to spend on four years regardless of expectations. The worst part is that this example is more affordable than many other schools so many are paying much, much more.

Wouldn't it be so much better if you could still get the same experience, the same education, the same degree without paying anything?

I think so. Hopefully you do too because now we start the fun stuff—grants and scholarships which <u>you do not have to pay back!</u>

Definition 3: Grants

Grants are often need-based and they do not have to be paid back. These are offered by the U.S. Department of Education and can be accessed by filling out the FAFSA. There are federal grants such as the Pell Grant as well as state-based grants. Additionally, some career paths such as teaching have grants because there is such a high need for teachers in some areas.

Definition 4: Scholarships

Scholarships are accessible to anyone and also do not need to be paid back. You can lose this money if you do not maintain a certain number of classes or fail to meet other criteria, but as long as you complete your degree and fill those criteria, you will never lose it or have to pay the money back.

Scholarships can be merit-based, meaning based on performance, whether it be academic, athletic, artistic, etc., and need-based, which are based on the student's financial situation. They can also be awarded by governments, universities, or private companies, organizations, and institutions.

University-based scholarships can also be either automatic or competitive. Automatic scholarships are awarded based on meeting certain requirements (e.g., a financial aid office could include a scholarship in your financial aid letter if you have a 3.75 GPA and a 28+ ACT score). You may think you need a 4.0 or a perfect SAT/ACT score in order to receive these but you'd be surprised! We found over 200 scholarships for students with a 3.5 or lower but it all depends on how open you are regarding universities.

One student, Tabitha, was a self-proclaimed average student. She and her mother assumed she'd never receive anything from a university because of her average GPA and test scores and were solely focusing on private scholarships. After going through our bonus lesson on merit scholarships in our online course, she decided to apply to another school and was awarded $34,000! As you can imagine, she jumped on the opportunity and enrolled immediately, shocked at how they just knocked off a huge chunk of the bill. Finding schools that offer you tens of thousands of dollars is a fast way to decreasing what you have to pay and making it easier to find private scholarships to cover the rest.

Alternatively, private scholarships will always be competitive, requiring some sort of submission or application. **This is a good thing** because we can increase our chances by increasing our competitiveness. It also helps us decipher if a scholarship is a scam or not. More on this later.

Another characteristic of scholarships is that they can either be one-time or recurring, also called renewable. What does this mean? If it's a one-time scholarship, it is for only one semester or school year. If it is recurring, it usually is awarded all 4 years or sometimes even 5! Most scholarships through universities are recurring, though you always want to confirm that. You should also always ask if the amount increases each year since tuition most likely will. For private scholarships, you can find both types. I had a mixture of both. Sometimes a recurring scholarship will require you to submit documentation each year in order to receive the following year's award.

"My daughter applied for 34 scholarships and won 10. She earned a total of $42,000 in scholarships!!! Some were one-time awards and others were renewable for a total of 4 years. The Scholarship System is a valuable springboard to applying for and ultimately winning scholarships."

– Eli, Father of 2 Students, Graduating Debt-Free
Over $100,000 in Scholarship Wins

How do you receive this money?

Grant money will be sent to your college and applied to your balance. With scholarships, it depends on the foundation or whoever is giving you the money. For the most part, I suggest having it sent directly to your school so that you are not tempted to cash it in. Also, you then know it is being applied to your massive bill that we calculated earlier.

IMPORTANT NOTE: Some universities limit how much they will allow you to receive, so if you hit this maximum, they will write you a check for any amount over your bill's balance and you can have any remaining scholarships sent directly to you instead. Either way, know that loan, grant, and scholarship money is almost always sent directly to your university, so you have to stay on top of them and ensure you are getting proper credit for what you have received.

Also, even if you receive enough scholarship money to completely cover your bill, you must "apply" the money to the bill by logging into your account and paying the bill with the credited funds. Do not assume because you received scholarship money that the bill is just taken care of. Lastly, in many cases you will still be offered student loans. Be careful not to accidentally accept these if you do not need them!! Financial aid award letters are tricky and word student loans as if they are an award or gift, which is not true since they accumulate interest and they have to be paid back! I once interviewed a sophomore in college who had blindly approved his entire financial aid package thinking it was all debt-free money to later discover $13,000 of it was student loans. He didn't even need that much! You will most likely have to check a box acknowledging that you are turning down any loans (which is a great thing!), but please be cautious when paying the bill.

Definition 5: Cash Awards

The last item I would like to cover is cash awards. The one thing that surprised me in college is that there are awards out there that are not scholarships but do not have to be paid back and are sent directly to you.

However, the reason they fit into this category is not just because they give you money but also because many are merit-based or competitive. You can be poor, rich, or in the median level and still be able to apply.

Some of these are a decent amount, too. I received $3,000 my senior year in college after my bills were already covered. That was okay because, like I said, it is not a scholarship. It is literally a 'cash' award, in the form of a check, to you for your leadership, community service, or some other criteria you have proven yourself in.

The other nice difference is that the money is awarded immediately upon winning, so in that specific semester, whereas scholarships are often for the following school year or semester.

These are typically a one-time award, never recurring.

The way to get these is to START building your competitiveness NOW and continue as soon as you get to college. You have to prove yourself for these but these are some of the best options out there. We will cover how to become competitive in Step 4!

Lessons Learned

Before we move on, let's recalculate how much college would cost you if you received scholarships. That was a trick—it would cost you NOTHING if you managed to bring in enough funding!

Doesn't that sound great? A four-year degree at the college of your choice that does not cost you a penny!

Now that we have covered the basics, we are about to get into the good stuff where you will find out how to pull that off.

Get excited!

Can you smell the money?

In a worst-case scenario, if you have to take out loans, try to take out the subsidized loans like I mentioned earlier because you do not pay any of the interest while you are in college. You can only get access to these if you and your parents fill out the FAFSA each year. If you have to take out a loan freshman year but get enough scholarships for the last three years, you may be able to save any excess scholarship money and pay off that loan right away rather than pushing it out and building expensive interest.

One of our students, Heather, managed to do this.

When she found us, she had already borrowed $9,000 for her freshman year in college. Then, after hearing me say that you can still win money even once you're already in college, she started The Scholarship System. By the end of freshman year, she had sophomore year covered. And by the end of sophomore year, she was going to have an overage check for junior year! Imagine if she just assumed she'd have to borrow every single year versus giving scholarships a shot. She would've borrowed $36,000 or more versus only $9,000. We'll talk more about how she did this but know she was actually a shy student and not very involved. She just had to figure out what her own selling points were and keep on applying!

There are multiple ways to pay for college, but we all like the idea of it being free. There are many different avenues to get scholarships, which we will discuss soon, but the key is to stay motivated.

So keep Step 1 in mind, where we covered your goals and accountability partners, Step 2, where we explained your different options, and get ready for Step 3, where we will find the perfect scholarships for YOU so that you can start winning that money.

Now we begin to cover the reason you wanted this book in the first place: how you can get a reduced bill, a free ride, or even get paid to go to school. This all depends on your level of dedication to The Scholarship System but I know you can do it. Otherwise, you would not have gotten this far in the book, especially after that painful last section of realizing how much college costs.

The Hunt Is On

Finding Scholarships That Have Little Competition
Yet Can Fund Your Free Ride

If you have made it to this point in the book, you are already ahead of at least half of your fellow student colleagues. Great job!

As we covered, being in the right mindset is what success really boils down to—not just in scholarships but in anything you pursue. If you can find the motivation and drive to push through whatever barriers you meet, you will be amazed at how much you can accomplish.

You are also armed with the basic financial aid knowledge so that when you are discussing financial aid with your guidance counselor or university, you will know what is going on so that you can make the decisions that are best for you, rather than signing up for years of debt bondage.
Now, let's talk about where you can find the scholarships. Remember that we want to get you funding that you **do not have to pay back.**

That includes three types: grants, scholarships, and cash awards. Grants can be found via the FAFSA, and this chapter is going to cover where to find scholarships and cash awards.

More specifically, we will discuss legitimate scholarships that actually apply to you and have less competition so your chances are much higher than one in a million.

First, we will go over what to look for in legitimate scholarships and how to scope out those scholarships that are worth your valuable time. Then we will go over where to look and how to find scholarships that do not have the whole country applying for them at the same time.

When to Apply for Scholarships: Increasing Your Chances by Applying When There Is Less Competition

Many students are surprised when I tell them they could have begun applying for scholarships as young as 4 years old. It's true! There are drawing competitions for young children where they can win a bond that matures when they go to college. Crazy, huh?

> *"Our 8th-grader earned her first cash award*
> *in February. $1,000 and it was the first scholarship*
> *she applied for!"*
>
> – David, Parent of Student in The Scholarship System

In reality, many of us don't start applying that young. Many students wait until senior year or later. If that's you, it's okay because I am here to tell you it's never too late. I continued applying every single year throughout college, bringing in more and more scholarship dollars to help cover any expenses I had. In fact, many of our students in The Scholarship System course are already in college and decided they wanted to avoid borrowing *more money*. One student who comes to mind, Heather, had to borrow $9,000 for her freshman year and then found us. After implementing the 6 steps you are learning in this book, she didn't have to borrow anything for sophomore year and then actually received an **overage check** for her junior year! Now imagine if she thought the game was over when she graduated from high school. She would have borrowed at least $36,000 instead of letting other people pay for her final three years through scholarships.

"I got a cash influx while studying abroad. It was amazing to not be constrained by money. It's never too late to apply."

– Brikken, Student, Received Over $80,000

That said, that doesn't mean to wait until college to start this process. Remember: Heather still had to borrow $9,000, which is nothing to balk at!

So when is the ideal time to apply for scholarships? Junior year. If I could, I'd have all students begin this process in their junior year. I know you're thinking, "But junior year is so busy!" and that is true; however, senior year will be just as busy if not even more so. And if we can put in the work in our junior year in high school, we will be able to reuse materials for the admissions process and scholarship applications during our senior year, making our life much easier when most students are so stressed over admissions and miss tons of scholarship deadlines because of it.

Again, if you are already a senior or older, that's okay! You still have plenty of time to apply. But you need to start NOW. Do not wait. And if you're a junior, don't procrastinate.

What about the most common deadline months?

Believe it or not, there are deadlines throughout the entire year for scholarships; however, certain times are certainly busier than others. October and December are major deadline months for scholarships. This means many students who wait until spring semester senior year already missed out on tons of scholarships.

Still, spring will have the busiest deadline months for the scholarship season. January through April are major deadline months, and the deadlines will go all through summer. In fact, through The Scholarship System, we've given out tens of thousands of dollars in scholarships over the last decade and our deadline isn't until mid-July each year!

Overall, we want to make sure we begin this process as early as possible but please know it's also never too late. If you begin this process and perhaps don't fully cover the first year of school, you can continue applying throughout college and receive more and more funding like I did.

Now that you know when to look, let's get into what to look for!

What to Look For: Navigating Your Way Through the Endless Scholarships Out There

When looking for scholarships, it is important to understand that any amount helps. I know it would be nice to get a $250,000 scholarship in one shot, but unfortunately, your competition thinks that as well. The nice thing is that we are going to show you how to find scholarships that still can result in a free ride but are actually reasonable to apply for. If you want to apply for the Coca-Cola scholarship or the KFC scholarship, each of which receives tens of thousands of applicants, you can still apply for everything else I am going to cover applying to. However, I am going to tell you right now that the chances of winning those are really, really slim compared to many others. Nevertheless, I wish you the best of luck and say shoot for the stars! But don't overlook the ones I am about to discuss.

Instead, what we are going to focus on are scholarships in odd places that have a few to zero applicants but give you a decent amount of money. These are usually $500-$5,000, but like I said, that adds up quickly.

So please disregard the dollar amount when you are applying. Don't look at a scholarship and say "Oh, that's only $500. That's not worth my time." Instead, think of all the things that $500 can buy such as all your groceries or textbooks that you normally have to pay for out of pocket. Or think about how many hours you would have to work to make that amount. If you're making $10/hour, you'd have to work 50 hours to earn $500. I promise you no scholarship will take 50 hours or even close to that amount of time. Remember Joseph? He won $600 after only 45 minutes of work thanks to what we'll cover in Steps 5 and 6. Another student, Jessica, spent two hours on an application for a study abroad scholarship and won $1,500—that's an hourly rate of $750! And believe me—there are many more stories like this.

> *"Amazing news, been working on scholarships all year with my oldest daughter. She got a $350, $2000, then a $3000, and just last month she was awarded a $20,000 over 2 years scholarships! Don't ever give up writing them as this proves it's all worth it!"*
>
> – Tracy, Mother of Student. Ended Up With An Overage Check by Junior Year

The next point I would like to make is that you should always read the criteria before putting tons of effort into a scholarship application. If the criteria say you must be a Florida resident with a 4.0 and own a dog but you don't meet any of those, do not apply! Your application will only be thrown in the trash. We are going to look for scholarships that specifically **apply to YOU** so that you have a good chance of winning them.

QUICK TIP

Sometimes, and I mean sometimes, criteria can be stretched **a bit**. Now I am not saying all the criteria can be thrown out the window, but here is one that I found: I applied for a scholarship that said high school students can apply. It was recurring, which means if you received the scholarship, you would get the award all four years as long as you still met the academic criteria such as a 3.5 GPA, at least 12 credit hours (4 classes) per semester, etc.

I was already a freshman in college and it didn't say high school students only or that college students cannot apply so I contacted them and asked if I could apply. They replied saying they didn't realize college students applied for scholarships (which you will, too, after reading this!) and that they'd be happy to consider my application. In the end, I received $4,000 per year and, if I wanted to stay an extra year, I would have gotten that fourth-year award as well since the funding didn't begin until my sophomore year in college.

"My daughter and I always had the desire to apply for scholarships but we needed this program to help us find the "right ones" and not waste our time on ones that seemed too good to be true. My daughter just received a $3000 scholarship this week that we did not even think she qualified for but pursued anyways with the knowledge from this program."

– Tracy, Mother of Daughter Who Ended with an Overage Check

If you have questions about one of the criteria, do not be shy—give them a call or send them an email to clarify. It never hurts to ask, but you will never get the money if you do not ask and apply. Also, you will be on their radar if you reach out to them with great questions and in a professional manner because you already displayed initiative.

One final tip here: please do the contacting yourself. It shouldn't be your parent or guardian. You're an adult (or will be one soon) and it will leave a much better impression if you contact the committee yourself. You can certainly have a parent, guardian, or teacher review the email beforehand but ultimately, it should come from YOU!

*"Applying for scholarships is like applying for jobs.
Most of the time, your application is thrown into a huge pool of other applications just like yours and unless you have a contact within the business, you may never hear back. The advice when applying to jobs is to have a connection introduce you or pass your name along. I found the same goes for scholarships.*

For every scholarship I won, I had reached out to the main contact with either a question about the application/deadline/supporting materials, or had made a comment saying thank you for letting me apply, I'm looking forward to hear back. By no means am I saying that I won every time I did this, but getting my name in their mind beforehand I believe made my application stand out and helped them to pay attention when it came in."

– Mackenzie Mylod, Student, Graduated College Debt-Free

Hide and Seek: Finding Scholarships Where No One Else Is Looking

As I said earlier, you can apply for those massive scholarships that everyone knows about. There is nothing wrong with that. They are just going to be much more challenging to win versus smaller, less-noticeable, less-competitive scholarships. We will now cover where to look for those that have less competition and how to find the ones that directly apply to you.

Here are some of the common places you can find scholarships:

1   **Books** – There are enormous books already created that are basically a directory for scholarships. One is called The Ultimate Scholarship Book, which is released each year. This book can be scary and overwhelming because it is literally over 800 pages, but if you go through and put tabs on the pages that have scholarships that apply to you, it will feel much more manageable. This book isn't the cheapest, but if you receive one scholarship, you have already paid for that book as well as this one. You can also just go to your local library, which most likely has multiple books of scholarships.

2   **School Office Filing Cabinets and Websites** – When I was in high school, my guidance counselors had a magical drawer of scholarships that were sent to their office or emailed to the counselors. Sometimes organizations and companies just send scholarship details to schools and rely on counselors to spread the word. Many high schools now put the scholarships on their website or in their student portal such as Blackboard or Naviance. Still, I highly suggest going to your guidance office and asking to see any scholarships they are aware of. I think you will be surprised at how many there are—and sometimes they don't get around to adding them to the website! By making it known that I was pursuing scholarships, my counselor sought me out a few times with some that passed through their office.

This isn't only for high school years! If you are already in college, or once you get to college, you can do the same thing with two different offices.

One is the financial aid office, which serves all students on campus. This office often considers you for scholarships upon admission but sometimes has money only available to upperclassmen, which means you would need to apply after the admissions process. Please note: if you are in the admissions process, not all colleges will automatically consider you for their scholarships. They may require a separate application from your admissions application. In fact, my alma mater did this! If I just applied to the university and didn't submit that separate university-based scholarship application, I wouldn't have received anything!

Beyond the financial aid office, you should also have a counselor or advisor specifically designated to your department or major who will know of even more scholarships. I received over $8,000 in scholarships through our business school and I only found out about the application because I stopped by and asked. In fact, they even told me they barely had any applications! A school of 4,000+ students and only a handful applied for the scholarship.

Make sure you talk to both offices to find out about potential scholarships through your university or college. These same offices may have some information online as well so feel free to look there first.

3 **Local Organizations** – Aside from school offices, another "office" that may be useful is that of a local organization. Local, civic organizations include Rotary Clubs, Elks Clubs, Kiwanis, Optimus Club, Knights of Columbus, and Lions Club but are certainly not limited to those.

We've had students receive scholarships from local lawyers, doctors, grocery stores, construction companies, dentists, banks, credit unions, community foundations, festivals, clubs like PTA or PTSA, and so much more. Some of these may list through your local high school but many will not. Brainstorm a few of the topics below and see if they offer scholarships in your area.

CLUBS I'M A PART OF:

PARENT/GUARDIAN EMPLOYER(S):

MY EMPLOYER:

MY DENTIST:

FAMILY BANK/CREDIT UNION:

LOCAL COMMUNITY FOUNDATION:

LOCAL WORKFORCE DEVELOPMENT BOARD:

 COURSE MEMBERS

For those who are members in The Scholarship System online course, we provide you with our annual Scholarship Source Guide with 100+ places to look for scholarships.

Lastly, I want to mention that for local clubs and organizations, you may be able to find national offices or parent offices that offer even more funding! For example, some fraternities or sororities may offer scholarships for their local chapter but also have some at the national level. Same with PTA/PTSA and honor societies.

4 **Scholarship Websites** – First and foremost, since the first edition of this book, we have spent the last decade creating endless free resources for families including blog posts, downloadable tools and worksheets, videos, webinars, live trainings, and more. You will find links to all our free resources at the end of this book. That said, one of your best places to go will be thescholarshipsystem.com. In fact, we release our own vetted scholarship lists on our website. You can find one of our latest lists at **www.thescholarshipsystem.com/scholarshiplist**.

When I was applying for scholarships, most counselors pushed me toward sites like Fastweb.com. While there certainly can be legitimate scholarships on these sites, there are also limitations.

First, that's where everyone goes so, naturally, they'll be more competitive. Second, the sites charge committees a fee to list their scholarships. For example, we've given out scholarships every year for nearly a decade through The Scholarship System but do not list them on these major search engines because we'd rather use that money for an additional scholarship! This means many scholarships out there are NOT on these search engines. Third, there are a ton of junk or scam scholarships on these websites so you need to know what you're looking for. Lastly, they'll probably flood whatever email you use when you sign up for their site.

Collegeboard.com can be a great source for not just scholarship applications but also more tips and tricks on applying. There are tons of search engines out there so just be careful that you do not waste your time.

There are always changes to the top sites (which we keep updated in our Scholarship System online course) but at the time of updating this book, here's our latest list of websites we approve of:

1. The Scholarship System
2. JLV College Counseling
3. Raiseme
4. Scholly
5. College Board Scholarship Search
6. Broke Scholar
7. Big Future (College Board)
8. CareerOneStop
9. Student Scholarships
10. Tuition Funding Sources

No matter what website you go to, you always have to keep an eye out for scams or sweepstake scholarships we don't want to waste our time on. I'll give you specific details on that shortly.

5 **The Scholarship System's Google Method** – This is my personal favorite. It seems so simple and I believe many people attempt this for at least a few minutes but not how we are about to do it. Of course, Google is just a way to find scholarships on other sites but this can be a powerful tool. Many scholarships that exist are on sites like the ones I listed above, but there are also many that are only on the company's homepage. This means that if you limit your search strictly to scholarship databases (whether in books or on scholarship sites), you can miss out on some massive cash opportunities.

In this section, we are going to fill out a worksheet that can help you come up with terms to Google in order to find scholarships that specifically pertain to you. They will be on foundations', companies', or organizations' sites rather than some major scholarship database.

The goal here is to uncover hidden scholarships with less competition. We'll do that by finding legitimate scholarships, directly linked from the sources' websites, and ones that aren't on those search engines, meaning only students who know this trick will find them!

To do so, we will develop phrases that you can search in Google. In the table below, fill in as many boxes as possible within each category.

Under 'List activities you are involved in,' list everything you do, whether it be something in school such as band or basketball or any other hobby such as scrapbooking, singing, public speaking, etc. It doesn't have to be official as in an organized club through your school. If you have a hobby or passion that you spend a lot of time on, on your own outside of school, write that down as well! The rest of the categories in the chart are pretty easy to understand.

Once you form this list, you can search each of those terms with the word 'scholarship' after it. For example, you can search scrapbooking scholarships, singing scholarships, public speaking scholarships—do you see where I am going with this? The list goes on. You can also reverse it by putting 'scholarships for' before the search term.

You can also search the same words but with 'awards' at the end: scrapbooking awards, singing awards, etc. If nothing comes up, try 'foundations' or 'organizations' and search on their sites for scholarships. Either way, this can lead you to many scholarships that you would never have found through the other sources we talked about. These are also the best ones to dig up because, if you could not find them through the popular methods, neither could your competition, which means a much higher chance of winning the big bucks.

Here are some specific examples to give you a better idea:

- Computer science scholarships
- Scholarships for computer science majors
- Scholarships for horse lovers
- Graphic design scholarships
- STEM scholarships for women
- Scholarships for magicians

Another great search is to specifically look for associations related to your desired trade, major, or career path. You can do that by adding the word 'association' to your search. Here are a few more examples:

- Marketing Association Scholarships
- Engineering Association Scholarships

Here is a quick story of how a current student in pharmacy school used a similar tactic to get scholarships:

"I narrowed down the traits which make me stand out and then used those keywords to search online. For instance, I am a pharmacy student, but I am also a first generation in the United States. So, I searched under 'pharmacy' and 'first generation' to increase my chances of finding fitting scholarships.

"Another strategy was to predict which corporations or brands would be more likely to give out scholarships and then search it online. For instance, Tylenol is a well-established company and gives out scholarships to students in the healthcare field. I discovered this through searching on Google whether Tylenol offers a scholarship."

– Anastasiya Plagova

The Savvy Scholarship Locator

Directions: Google the keyword you write below + the word 'scholarship' or 'cash award.' If you do not find anything, try searching your keyword + 'foundation' or 'organization.' You can then look on the organizations' sites for scholarships.

You do not have to limit yourself to this table. I found many of my scholarships by sitting on Google and trying to come up with any combination possible that could lead me to a scholarship. Be creative and see where it takes you!

Now here's the most important part of this process that is very important for you to understand: how to know which search results to focus on.

When you type phrases like the ones above, your first results will be sites that largely pay to be at the top or are large search engines like scholarships.com or fastweb.com. While you can take a look at these, where we want to focus our time is on the actual scholarship providers' sites. For example, a marketing association may be offering scholarships to marketing students on their own website. The URL would be something like www.marketingassociation.com/scholarships (this is just a made-up example to make the point). We want to skip fastweb.com and other search engine sites and instead go directly to the provider's webpage. We can then get a feel for the scholarship provider. Is it a legitimate website? Organization? Does it look like I can trust them? This discernment is important to avoid wasting time on scams, but if done correctly, you can uncover dozens of scholarships that aren't even on the search engines and therefore have less competition!

While working with families over the last decade, this has been our most effective method for uncovering scholarships students can actually win. Does it take more time than just filtering a few criteria on those search engine websites? Absolutely. However, this method improves your chances of receiving scholarship dollars by first, making sure the scholarship is legitimate, second, finding ones that aren't listed on search engines and therefore are less competitive, and third, are actually tailored to your eligibility since you're selecting the search terms based on your own involvements, characteristics, passions, and interests. This method is simple but not easy. *Don't underestimate the power of The Scholarship System's Google Search Method.*

6   **Social Media Sites** – This wasn't as common when I was applying but I will tell you that there are a ton of scholarships on social media sites these days. In fact, if you go to our website (thescholarshipsystem.com) as well as follow The Scholarship System on Facebook, Instagram, YouTube, Pinterest, and other social platforms, you will find we share tons of scholarship lists throughout the year. The great thing about our lists is that we've already vetted the scholarships for you.

 COURSE MEMBERS

Course members get access to our members-only Facebook group where we share scholarships weekly.

You can search for any profiles with 'scholarship' in their name and find dozens, if not hundreds, that come up. You can also look up #scholarship on the various social platforms. It never hurts to look here so I say give it a shot! Just make sure you've put your main focus on our Google Search Method and going through our website before spending too much time on other social platforms. We want to make sure you're using your time wisely!

Savvy Scholarship Locator

List activities you are involved in	List organizations you are a part of	List characteristics that are unique to you	List groups that you believe would fund scholarships	List companies you love or are passionate about	List areas or subjects you believe you are strong in
Ex. Public Speaking	Ex. Ronald McDonald House	Ex. Oldest of five siblings or first-generation student	Ex. Coaches	Ex. Walmart	Ex. Leadership, community service, arts, sciences, etc

Spotting Scholarship Scams

I've met families where their student applied to "dozens and dozens of scholarships and never heard back," and when I ask to see which scholarships they applied to, 9 times out of 10, many are scams or sweepstake scholarships. Let's quickly dissect which scholarships you want to look out for so that you don't waste time on the WRONG scholarships (like I did my junior year in high school). If you've been applying to these, don't worry—most of us have. But now, because you're using this book, you won't fall victim to them any longer!

The 'good' sites have thousands of scholarships on them that have competitive criteria and require essays or some sort of submission material. If you find a site that says, *'Fill out your information and you can be randomly selected for a scholarship,'* that site or scholarship is probably not legitimate. We call this the "Scholarship Spectrum." On one end, you have easy, quick, minimal applications. These take 15 minutes or less to submit. On the other end, you have ones that require materials like essays, transcripts, recommendation letters, and more. As you can imagine, these require more time up front; however, they are much more worth your time because you actually have a chance of winning money.

Identifying Legitimate Scholarships

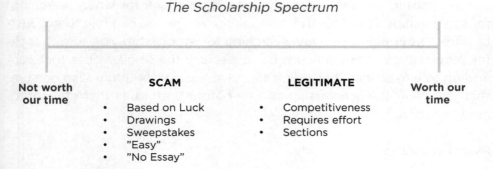

The Scholarship Spectrum

Not worth our time	SCAM	LEGITIMATE	Worth our time
	• Based on Luck	• Competitiveness	
	• Drawings	• Requires effort	
	• Sweepstakes	• Sections	
	• "Easy"		
	• "No Essay"		

If you truly want to receive scholarships, they are going to take more work than random drawings so please do not fall for that. Drawings and sweepstakes sites are just trying to collect your information and send you spam emails. In fact, the email I used for these is completely destroyed—I had to create a new one because of how much spam I was receiving! Instead, we want to find scholarships on the other end of the spectrum that will take more time up front but actually can result in money for college.

Now this might sound like it'll take way more work than you expected but in reality, this is a good thing! When applying for scholarships based on competitiveness, you can actually increase your chances of winning, which we'll cover in Steps 4 and Step 5. Things are more within your control versus ones that are just based on luck. Also, in Step 6, we'll teach you tricks to save time so that it doesn't have to take a ton of time as you continue applying.

Prior to applying for a scholarship, ask yourself, "Is this based on luck or is this based on my competitiveness?" If your answer is luck, avoid it! Even if it takes less than 15 minutes, doing 10 of those could have instead been a phenomenal, reusable essay for a legitimate scholarship that actually resulted in money!

Recap

In this chapter, we went over what you should look for when searching for scholarships as well as the main places where you can find them. Just to refresh your memory, when searching for scholarships, be sure to look for scholarships of any amount but especially the smaller ones that can add up to a free ride. These typically have less competition. Also be sure that you meet the scholarship criteria before putting all that effort into applying for it.

Places you can search include:

- Scholarship books that you can buy or check out at the library
- Offices and websites such as your counselor's office at high school or college as well as offices of local organizations such as the Rotary Club
- Popular scholarship search engines, though proceed with caution!
- Google using our Google Keyword Method and Savvy Scholarship Locator
- Social media sites such as Facebook, Instagram, Pinterest, and more
- The Scholarship System website and social media profiles

Action Item

Before we move on to the next chapter, please find 5 scholarships from any of our sources and look at the applications. To make the best use of your time, make sure they are scholarships that you can actually apply for like we talked about at the beginning.

Next, write down what areas the applications ask about. For example, do they ask about your leadership experience? If so, write down 'leadership.' Do they ask about community service involvement?

If so, write down 'community service.' This will help us in the next chapter where we find ways that you can both become a competitive candidate in the future as well as tailor what you have already done in life to sell yourself immediately.

Now let's use this to make you a competitive candidate and help you start winning that scholarship money!

"Thank you for your system. It was the kick in the rear and inspiration that we needed. My son secured 3 scholarships this spring, totaling $6,500. I'm grateful for the heavenly guidance that pointed me in your direction. I'm not sure we would have felt so empowered without your help."

– Alane, Mother of Student Who Secured Free Ride

Saving and Documenting Scholarships

When searching for scholarships and building your list, one of the most important steps after ensuring they're legitimate is documenting them. Many times, students and parents or guardians find a ton of great scholarships only to forget about them and miss the deadlines! We don't want this to happen to you. In this bonus chapter, we are going to cover a few options. Feel free to choose the best method for you!

This is focused on documenting scholarships you want to apply for. Later on, we'll discuss documenting materials you will submit.

Documenting Scholarships

 The Scholarship System App & Chrome Extension: After years of watching students miss deadlines, we decided to create an app to help you. This isn't like the search engine apps out there loaded with outdated scholarships that don't pertain to you. Instead, it's actually blank inside, waiting for you to input the scholarships YOU want to apply to. This way you know every single scholarship in your app is one you already vetted and chose to apply for.

There are a lot of great benefits of using the app and Chrome Extension. First, it alerts you when deadlines are coming up. Second, you can document requirements. Third, your parent or guardian can add scholarships into it as well so you can tag team the process!

To learn how to use this free tool we created for you, just go to **www.thescholarshipsystem.com/app**. It's available for iPhone and Android but you can also use it from your computer.

2   **College Cost Calculator Spreadsheet (Scholarship Tracker Tab):** Course members have access to the full benefit of our College Cost Calculator, which includes a tab to track scholarships.

3   **Create your own spreadsheet:** I do recommend having some sort of digital file versus only using paper or bookmarking websites. Having a summary can give you the ability to plan ahead, get a quick idea of deadlines coming up, and skim through requirements if you document those as well. If creating your own spreadsheet, some columns I'd recommend creating include but are not limited to:

    a. Name of Scholarship
    b. URL
    c. Deadline
    d. Dollar Amount
    e. Renewable or not?
    f. If different, application URL
    g. Login Info
    h. Submitted or not?
    i. Received or not?
    j. Requirements

You can get as granular as you want when creating your spreadsheet. If you want a different column for each type of requirement, you can do that too. That said, don't make it so complicated that you don't actually use it.

4 **Now here is the most important step:** set electronic reminders to check your sheet regularly and/or for each scholarship's deadline. Again, this is why we created The Scholarship System App and Chrome Extension—we found many families create a great list but then forget to check it and miss deadlines. Do not let this happen to you! Always set electronic reminders for deadlines.

5 **Print them out and organize them in a binder.** For those who love paper, this is also acceptable and a method I've seen used in conjunction with our app so they have electronic reminders but also a physical copy. I recommend organizing the binder by due date so you can quickly jump to the ones you need to focus on in the upcoming month. No matter what, you will need a digital component to go with this since you'll need copies of essays, resumes, transcripts, etc., but at least this can be a physical reminder of the applications you want to submit. I highly recommend having the binder somewhere you constantly see it!

Heating Up Your Application

Successful Strategies for Becoming a Competitive Candidate

In the last chapter, we discussed where you can uncover scholarships that not only fit your qualifications but also have less competition so that you have a good chance of winning them. **This is half the battle!**

In this chapter, we are going to get specific. This will lay the foundation for writing award-winning scholarship essays.

First, we are going to cover successful strategies in building your qualifications so that you can be even more competitive when applying.

I bet some of you are thinking, "But I am already a senior in high school! I don't have enough time to get new stuff on my resume!" First, I want to say that is false. You can, and should, START NOW no matter what year you are in. As I mentioned probably too many times now, you can apply until your junior or senior year in **college**. This means that, unless you are graduating **college**, it is NOT too late for you!

Secondly, I am going to show you how we can tailor what you have been doing the last couple of years to fit these competitive areas that scholarship committees are asking about. This means that, even if you are a senior in high school, this chapter will help you.

Are you ready to supercharge your application? I will tell you now — you will be shocked at how awesome you will sound by the end of this chapter.

To start off, we have another worksheet to help you. In the one below, we are going to brainstorm new things you can begin to get involved with in order to meet the scholarships' criteria you found at the end of the last chapter.

Here is how to fill out this chart. I've included an example in the first row.

1   **Competitive Area** – Write the criteria topic you found on your applications (leadership, community service, jobs, etc.). What are they asking about in their questions? What areas are there on a resume?

2   **Current Experience** – Write down anything you have done in the past that you believe fits this subject. Do not be afraid to brag here. If you have eight different experiences in which you believe you exemplified leadership skills, write them all down. If you assisted people in any genuine way without pay, put that down as community service. We will talk more about how to fill these out in the next section.

3   **New Experience** – Try to think of areas where you can add involvement in your key application areas. One tip here is to make sure you would actually be interested in the activity. You do not want to sign up for activities just because you want to put them in your application. This will show right through when judges are reading your essays. If you are passionate about something, this will also show and will give you much more kudos in your application. Once again, we will talk more about this next.

4   **Who you can talk to about beginning NOW** – This should be anyone involved already. It could be a teacher who runs a club in that area, a mentor or adult who does the same thing, or a friend or classmate who also does the activity. You can talk to them about what the activity is, when you would meet, how to get signed up and, most importantly, whether or not they enjoy it.

5   **When you will contact them** – Set yourself a strict deadline and stick to it. As you see in my hint, you want to start NOW so set your deadline for as soon as possible but still keep it realistic, otherwise you won't do it.

Now take five minutes and fill out the chart below. If you found more than three areas the scholarships are asking for, grab a sheet of paper and continue the table.

Competitive Candidate Chart

Key Competitive Area	Current experience in this area	New experience you can achieve in this area	Who you can talk to about beginning NOW	When you will contact this person by (hint: ASAP)
Ex) Leadership	Head of shift during the blood drive	Lead/start a committee in student council	President of student council	The next school day

Your chart should not be blank at this point. You should at least have the first column filled out based on what you discovered when looking up scholarship applications. It is okay if you do not have the second and third columns filled out because, in this next section, we are going to go over in detail ways you can fill them out with legitimate experiences. In the end, once this is filled up, you will have the foundation you need for your scholarship essays and applications.

Getting Involved Now

I want to begin by confronting most students' main doubt right off the bat. Many of you think, *It is too late to get involved.* By now, I am sure you can predict what I am going to say but I am going to tell you again anyway: START NOW, it is never too late.

If you are a freshman in high school, or even a junior in high school, you can begin building your competitiveness right away. You will be ahead of the game, which is great!

If you are a senior in high school or if you are already in college, you can use this too!

It is never too late.

Why? I know this is shocking, but graduating high school does not mean you are done for in the scholarship process. You can continue applying for four more years, so if you have not already built your credentials, start now. You may need loans your freshman year, but if you follow this book, you should not have to take any out by your senior year, or maybe sooner. Each year that I was in college, my scholarship balance grew and grew because I continued to apply as the years went on. You can too! Which also means you have time to build your competitiveness for scholarship applications.

Ways to Get Involved <u>That Count</u>

My first and most important suggestion is that you must do something you are interested in. Do not just join an organization because you want to have something for your scholarship applications; do it because you are interested in it.

Begin by joining a club that catches your eye. This is applicable for high school and college students. Most schools have organization fairs where groups can tell students about what they do. Find out when the next one is. If it has already passed, ask your counselor to see a list of all the student groups and contact either their president or advisor for more information. Organizations are always looking for more members, especially **involved members.**

If you do not see anything that interests you, start something! Ask your counselor how to begin a student organization. You will most likely need to find an advisor but this is a great experience that shows judges that you take initiative.

Perhaps you do not want to get involved in student groups. Before thinking of alternatives, I suggest giving it a shot and joining at least one because you can learn many useful skills from your interactions in these groups. However, there are always alternatives. Another way to 'get involved' that can supplement a lack of student organizations would be working on your own business. Have an idea? Start it! It does not have to make tons of money or even anything at all, but once again, this aligns with showing initiative here and you will learn an insane amount of skills. I promise.

We have covered some general suggestions but now let's get specific.

Here are the areas I frequently see on applications:

- **Leadership**
A great way to gain leadership is by joining an organization or team of some sort and taking on responsibility. You do not have to be the president right away, but try to take initiative and lead something.

For example, many student councils plan school dances, pep rallies, and blood drives. A great way to show you are a leader is to take a specific task that requires multiple people and head it. Do they need to organize a photographer and set up a specific area to take photos? Grab a team and take care of it. This counts! Are you part of a football team that can use some practice running through the plays? Take initiative and set up some meeting times.

I want to mention one more way you can gain leadership experience and that is a part-time job. Part-time jobs are highly respected because we all know it is tough to balance school and work. The best part? You get paid while gaining great qualifications.

When working at a part-time job, there may be situations where you have to lead your shift or make sure everyone completes their tasks before clocking out. Sometimes you have to multi-task and be resourceful because someone did not come in for their shift. These are all challenges where you utilize leadership skills and are absolutely fair game when writing your scholarship essays. So find somewhere that will hire you and hop on the experience train to success! It does not have to be a glorified job or the place where you will start your career but anything helps (and it is always nice to get paid).

In summary, anything you do that requires initiative and the ability to guide or work with others can be considered leadership, especially if you have respectfully taken the reins and completed the task as a group. Here are some skills you gain by being a leader:

*HINT: This will help in your essays. I will also have a major list at the end of the book for you.

Benefits of Leadership Experience	
Delegation skills	Confidence
Communication skills	Responsibility
Multi-tasking	Management skills
Time management	Problem-solving skills

What other skills do you gain by leading? Take just a few minutes to fill out the chart now. We will come back to this when discussing how to write an essay.

_____

_____

_____

_____

Now that we have gone over how to get involved and build leadership experience, start filling out the third column in your chart at the beginning of the chapter if you have 'leadership' as one of your topics.

If you get stuck, ask someone else you know who is very involved. Perhaps you can bring in your accountability partner here. I am sure they will have some suggestions!

• Community Service

Another area that is commonly mentioned on applications is community service. Community service is a great way to grow as a person but it is most obviously an excellent way to give back to the people and communities around you. One thing to remember is that community service is anything where you have contributed to a group without receiving pay.

So please do not disregard things you have done just because they were not with a major volunteer group.

What you do want to make sure of is that you enjoy what you are doing! This is where it gets fun. You can get major credit for having an impact on your community, peers or even large groups and yet you can just be doing something you love.

Here are some examples:

Do you like cooking? Cook a meal for a low-income family or for families who have sick children at the Ronald McDonald House.

Do you like playing guitar? Volunteer to play at a nursing home or for a children's hospital.

Do you enjoy making crafts? Sew blankets for a charity organization.

Do you like playing sports? Volunteer at a summer camp or Special Olympics.

I can go on forever. Just think of something you enjoy doing and creatively come up with ways you can involve that activity with helping people.

Here are some benefits you gain through community service:

Benefits of Community Service	
Build relationships	Meet diverse groups of people
Communication skills	Learn to be adaptable
Ability to motivate others	Learn to be persistent

NOTE: Many of the benefits of leadership and community service can be interchangeable.

What other skills do you gain by volunteering? Take another five minutes to fill out the chart.

_____

_____

_____

_____

Now take a few more minutes and fill out the first table in the chapter with activities you think you can do in order to build your volunteering experience if you had that as one of your scholarship criteria.

At this point, your table should be getting pretty full.

Gaining experience in these main areas certainly helps your chances of winning scholarships. You will be shocked at how applicable just these two areas can be to any essay or interview question. If there is a topic that we did not cover, just go through the same process in coming up with ways to build your credentials. Be creative in how you can meet the requirements and, as long as you can justify them and truly say you learned, were challenged, took initiative, etc., the scholarship committee will appreciate your response.

So, once again, it does not matter if you are a freshman in high school or a sophomore in college, you should get started in these areas right away.

The next section covers how you can tailor what you have already accomplished to fulfill these application requirements. Yes, getting involved is important, but I am sure you have some other activities on your plate that are pretty awesome already. Now we are going to teach you how to sell them.

Selling What You Have Already Accomplished

We realize you are already a rock star. Let's show the committee that.
Are you already a senior in high school? Do you need activities to write on your scholarship application but you are out of time (for this year) to start getting involved? This section is perfect for you!

Believe me, I know how it feels to look at a scholarship application and say, "Oh no, what can I put here?" but you will be surprised at how easy it can be to tailor something you have already done and show how awesome you are! You may have just overlooked it because it's a day-to-day activity for you.

You are probably already very busy. Perhaps you are constantly involved in something but you just do not know how to sell it, or perhaps you have not really been too involved but you know you have done a few great things that should count.

In this section, we will explain how to uncover activities that perhaps you did not realize were worth sharing and teach you how to sell these activities so that scholarship committees give you just as much credit as those you are competing against.

Welcome to selling 101 because that is basically what you are doing—you are selling yourself. Do not be afraid to toot your own horn because this is where it is OK to do so!

Tailoring Your Accomplishments to Meet Scholarship Criteria

Let's bring out those common topics:

- Leadership
- Community Service
- Academics

These areas all have very typical responses that most students think they must include. Many students assume leadership means they have to be president of something, community service means they have had to be involved in the blood drive or some other nationally recognized organization for years and academics means you have to have a 4.0.

Let me tell you that THESE ARE NOT THE ONLY WAYS TO ROCK THESE SECTIONS!

There are so many other ways you can sell yourself and still be a leader or a contributor to the community or someone who does well in academics or have made a special impact somehow. Essays are meant to show the skills you have learned, challenges you have overcome and the preparation you have gained for the future.

This is where we will fill out column 2 in the chart from the last section: *'Current experience in this area.'* Let's begin.

Leadership – You do not need a title to be a leader

Leadership experience does not mean you have to have a leadership position. I know that sounds like craziness but it is true. It can be anything where you led a group—even if it is only a few people.

We talked about this earlier but any time where you have taken initiative and guided a group is leadership. This includes committees, group projects, activities with your siblings, and more.

Were you in charge? Did you have to accommodate others' opinions while guiding the group to a common goal? Were you facing a major challenge for the group and had to use your problem-solving skills to come up with a solution? Oh yeah—that sounds good, doesn't it?

Now don't get me wrong. Judges love to see that you have held a position in one of your student organizations so that can certainly be a goal of yours, but do not think that you have to in order to write that you have leadership experience.

Here are some situations that would enable you to write about leadership experience:

Sports teams	Study groups	Challenging home situations
Academic teams	Volunteering activities	Working with siblings
Class projects	School activities	Babysitting

Have you been involved in anything listed above? Then I promise that you can write a great essay explaining how you have led a group, the lessons you learned, and the skills you gained, thus preparing you for college and future success. I promise that you can win scholarships with these activities that you have already done.

Here are ways to analyze what you have already accomplished and see if you can use it in an essay. The goal is to think of a few situations that you can reuse in your essays. We will talk more on writing later. This is just to get your mind going.

- Have you been part of any team where you helped make an executive decision and moved the team forward? Did you have to motivate the group to follow your decision?

- Did you have to coordinate others in order to complete a group project or class assignment? Did you organize a group to study for a test so that you all achieved success together?

- Have you volunteered? Did you lead the group in any way? Were there challenges your group faced for which you came up with a solution?

- Do you ever help out in the school's office? The guidance office? In class?

- Have you learned skills that will help you in college and your career?

- Do you have any challenging home situations? Do you have a sick family member whom you choose to help out a lot?

- Do your parents work a lot? Has this made you take on extra responsibility? Can you say that this taught you any valuable life lessons or prepared you for your future?

- Do you have many siblings that you help with? Do you coordinate them so that they are not running all over the place? Do you babysit and do the same thing?

If you said yes to any of the questions above, **you already have great experience that can get you scholarship money!**

I know everyone gets worried when it is senior year and they think time has run out for gaining experience for scholarship applications but you can turn many of the experiences you have had into responses on your applications.

Community Service – Yes, it counts if it was for a smaller organization or group

Now it is time to do the same for volunteer questions.

- Have you helped out a grandparent or neighbor where you did not get paid but helped them do something they were not able to do without your help?

- Did you mow the lawn for someone because they were sick or had surgery and could not do it themselves?

- Have you found stray animals and helped find them homes? Have you visited an animal shelter and helped take care of the animals in any way?

Think of things that you have done selflessly to help others. If you did not get paid, it was most likely something you could talk about in questions regarding volunteering and community service.

Academics – No, you do not have to be valedictorian to get scholarships

The last topic I want to discuss is academics. Many scholarship applications ask for your GPA, SAT and ACT scores, class ranking, etc. These are all surrounding your academic and testing experience so far.

If you have managed to pull off all A's and you got a great score on the SAT and ACT, that is great. Supplement that with some volunteering, extracurricular activities, and/or a part-time job and you are golden. That said, if you have a great GPA but have zero activities to show for your time beyond your classes, this can actually be more detrimental than having a less-than-perfect GPA. Committees want to see well-rounded students as they tend to succeed in college and beyond. So if you have high scores but you spend all your time studying and that's it, it's time to add something else to your calendar!

Alternatively, for those of you who perhaps struggled through your freshman year and have not been able to pull up your GPA, you can still earn scholarship money as well!

Yes, you heard me right. If you are not a straight-A student or have less than a 4.0 GPA, you can still receive financial aid. It will not be as easy as if you were a straight-A student but it is still possible.

How? Well, let me tell you.

First, many scholarships don't even look at GPA or they have requirements that are on the lower end like 2.8 or 3.2. We've given out scholarships for nearly a decade through The Scholarship System and we've never once used GPA as a factor in our decision.

For those that do factor in scores and GPA, there can be a way around this. Many scholarship applications leave room for an 'anything else you want the committee to know' essay. Please <u>never leave this blank!</u> This is your opportunity to wrap up your entire application and really sell yourself. This is also where you can justify your lower-than-4.0 GPA.

Justifying less-than-perfect grades or test scores

If you have terrible grades, low standardized test scores, and you do not do anything but play video games, I cannot help you. You've got to help yourself first and get out of the rut by joining something and improving your scores. However, if you have average grades and test scores, you especially need to be involved or have a part-time job. The only justifications for lower grades are perhaps special challenges you have faced and/or extra involvement outside of the classroom that takes time away from studying. Now I am not saying you should write every excuse in the book, but you can certainly explain why the scores are not where you want them to be <u>and how you are trying to correct this</u>. You cannot just simply admit that they are less than average and that is just where they are going to stay. You have to show that you have taken initiative to increase them and will continue to do so.

If you explain that you have lower scores and haven't studied as much as you would have liked, you should have a reason for that <u>as well as a remedy</u>. For example, explain (if it is true) that it is due to a part-time job and involvement with some volunteer group; however, you have recently designated a specific number of hours toward homework and studying only so that you can bring up your grades and test scores. Or you can explain that you have taken on especially challenging courses where you knew you would not get an A but decided to take the more challenging route so that you are truly prepared for college.

There are many ways to spin a less-than-perfect GPA or test score. Just be careful that you do not sound like you are just making excuses and genuinely come up with a way to remedy it.

I recently met a student in this exact situation. His father shared that his son's GPA is not where it needs to be. I asked if there was anything that happened to cause a lower GPA. His son then explained he started a design business and ended up swamped with clients. He was staying up late at night to deliver projects on time and was getting paid for them! Honestly, I was impressed. He told me he has taken on fewer clients so that he can try to raise his GPA. This is a great story and will be even better if he can show he got all A's and B's (or better) in the latest semester. We aren't trying to make excuses, but some committees can look past a low GPA or test score if there is a justifiable reason and a genuine effort to improve it.

Recap

In this chapter, I covered ways to gain experience, get involved, and build your credentials so that you can knock scholarship essays and applications out of the park.

I also covered strategies to explain what you have already experienced so that you can still write an amazing essay even if you have run out of time to gain more involvement. This is especially useful for you seniors who are about to graduate.

Lastly, I covered academics and how being a straight-A student is wonderful, but if you are not a straight-A student, you can justify this and still be a competitive scholarship applicant.

To narrow all this down to one main point, I showed how nearly every student can earn scholarship money. You just have to know how to build yourself in areas where you may need more experience and know how to sell what you have already done so far.

Now there is no excuse for not receiving scholarship money, so let's start applying!

Before you move on, please make sure that you have filled in all the tables in the chapter. This will be especially helpful when writing your essays, so make sure to come up with as many strategies, experiences, and benefits as possible.

In the next chapter, we are going to cover a basic system for applying for scholarships and then how to write a killer essay in minimal time that can be reused to win scholarship after scholarship.

Crushing Scholarship Applications One at a Time

In the last chapter, we discussed how to get involved as well as how to show that you are a competitive candidate with things you have already done. In this chapter, we are going to take that and cover how to apply for the scholarships with your newfound (or maybe it was already there) competitiveness. This chapter will be broken down into four sections:

1. Choosing Your Process – Guaranteeing success through an organized routine
2. Finding the best scholarships for YOU
3. Blasting through the application, one section at a time
4. Packaging – Putting your best foot forward through presentation

This chapter is extremely important. It wraps up everything we have covered and puts it into actionable items so that you can deliver a finished application that is ready to win.

Choosing Your Process – Guaranteeing Success Through an Organized Routine

The one guaranteed error students often make that will ensure tons of debt is <u>not applying</u>. But what stops students from applying? There are many reasons, I am sure; however, the main reason is that they miss the deadlines or did not manage to pull everything together correctly. So how can you avoid this to make sure you win scholarships? One major step forward is by simply creating a set process to prevent you from falling into these issues.

Here are some suggestions regarding your scholarship process, although there are certainly different ways depending on your personality and preferred work environment. With these tips, you will begin streamlining and simplifying the scholarship process and turning it into a, well, system.

1   **Keep all documents, recommendation letters, resume versions, essays, etc., in one safe place.**
You can certainly go the traditional way and use actual folders, but today you can also do this in a cloud-based storage site such as Dropbox or Google Drive. The benefit of this is that you can access your information anywhere. Do <u>not</u> just leave your files on your computer because if it crashes, you will lose everything. Believe me—I am speaking from experience here.

Create clearly defined folders so that you know where to find everything. Also, never delete anything. If you are creating a new version, save it as "Name _ V2" then "Name_V3," and so on and so forth so that you can always backtrack if you need to.

I kept everything throughout my scholarship process and reused the essays over and over. You never know when you will need them so make sure to keep it all organized.

2   **Create calendar reminders for deadlines.**
We covered documenting scholarship lists in the bonus chapter after Step 3. Many people now use the electronic calendars on their phones, computers, or in their email, but just remember to use a tool where you can set some sort of reminder so that you do not miss the deadlines. Whatever your strategy is for school, use the same one for scholarship applications. Deadlines vary from summertime to fall to spring so be sure to keep that information

available! Do not rely on you "remembering" to check your scholarship list regularly. Use technology to your advantage!

3 **Utilize your accountability partners in your process.**
Try to set scheduled meetings, even if they are only 5-15 minutes long. Accountability buddies are very useful and are excellent at ensuring you carry through and do not miss deadlines. Be sure to involve them in your entire process.

4 **Set up a separate email account strictly for scholarship applications.**
This keeps your applications and login information all in one place and keeps your personal email from being flooded with scholarship emails. Additionally, having an email dedicated to the scholarship process keeps your focus strictly on scholarships rather than other emails you are receiving.

5 **Set aside a specific time that you will always use strictly for applying for financial aid.**
Some people like to do their research and applying on a Saturday; others like to do it in the morning during the week. Whatever you prefer, try to set a consistent time frame where you will focus on the scholarship process. As I mentioned earlier, 40 hours a semester will be perfect for your process so try to factor that number into your timing. Either way, you want to make sure you actually carry through with the process. I'll explain more on this in the chapter for parents and guardians—they can certainly help you here if you want!

Finding the Best Scholarships for YOU

In Step 3, you found five different scholarships for which you met the specific criteria. If you didn't, I suggest pausing now and going back to that chapter to do so. If you still do not feel like you found anything, visit the Savvy Scholarship Locator worksheet, which will further help you in finding possible scholarship opportunities.

We have already covered this topic but here is a quick recap of the main characteristics you want included in the scholarships you are applying for:

1 Legitimate source: Make sure this is not just a random drawing or scam to collect your information. They also should not charge a fee to apply (memberships can be different).

2 Reasonable criteria for you: Do not waste time on applications that have requirements you cannot fill. If borderline, remember to reach out!

3 Deadline has not passed: I know this is obvious, but still, I just wanted to point out that scholarships close when they say they will close. If you really want to apply for this scholarship, set a reminder for about 8-10 months after the closed deadline so that you can apply next year. Remember—the scholarship process is not just a one-time thing. It is ongoing until you graduate college so you can certainly apply next time.

4 Any dollar amount: Remember that small dollar amounts quickly add up. Those $500-$2,000 scholarships have less competition because other students think these are not worth applying for. Any amount helps, so do not ignore a scholarship based on dollar amount.

Blasting Through the Application, One Section at a Time

There are five main areas of scholarship applications. The requirements certainly vary but this should cover at least 80% of what you will see.

1. General information section

This is where the scholarship committee gathers:

- Contact information

- University you plan to attend (this is just to get an idea so do not be afraid to list one you haven't applied to yet)

- Cost estimate of planned university—you can use the table from Chapter 2 because you want to make sure to include all costs, not just tuition.

- Scholarships already received

- Intended major (once again, this is okay to change after the fact unless it is part of the requirements)

- Current classes you are enrolled in

- Family history such as number of siblings, salary information, and parent information

- FAFSA information such as your Estimated Family Contribution (EFC) or, as of 2024, Student Aid Index (SAI)

This section should not take too much effort, but the one point I would like to make is that you should always make sure everything is filled out, spelled correctly, and is as accurate as possible. Applications can be thrown away without the essays even being read if the basic information section is filled out incorrectly.

You may have noticed that cost of your university and any scholarships already received are listed. The scholarship committees want to weigh in your need depending on the price of your higher education. It would be helpful to just keep this information in a spreadsheet or Word document so that you have it available for your applications in the future. Little tricks like this is where we begin to save time! It might not seem like much at the beginning, but as you continue to apply, it'll snowball into quite a bit of time saved.

2. Involvements

Many scholarship applications ask you to list any organizations or extracurricular activities you are involved in, whether they are athletic, religious, academic, etc. It is helpful to keep another Word document with this information because you will have to share this more often than not.

 COURSE MEMBERS

You have access to our Student Activities Worksheet to update after each semester and refer to for each application. This was my personal form used when I was going through the process.

When filling out this section, please do not forget our most recent chapter about selling what you have already done. You will be amazed at what you can list here. Do not think that you have to be president or treasurer in order to list your involvement. If you made a serious contribution, you can and should list it. If you are not sure what to put here, go back to the last chapter and reread it.

TIP: As you get involved, keep one file with the name of the organization, the date you got involved, and then any leadership or volunteer experiences within it. You should also keep track of any awards you have received such as honor roll, leadership recognitions, etc. I learned this the hard way but it is easy to forget everything you have done over the last few years! This is also where a parent or guardian may be able to help. More on that in the bonus parent chapter!

3. Essays

Now here is where you can make or break your scholarship application. I explained earlier that you do not have to be president of your organizations, you do not need a 4.0 GPA, but one thing you do need is a killer essay that sells what you have accomplished.

This section is going to go into detail because I want you to succeed and, if we can get a few good essays that you can reuse for your applications, you will be at least 80% where you need to be in order to get funding!

Before we go into my suggestions, here is what another recent graduate had to say about writing essays:

"Writing an essay takes a lot of time but once you finish it, you can usually just make small tweaks and use it for various applications. I would say I probably wrote about 10 over the years that I used on many different occasions. One essay normally took about 3-4 hours from start to end, and I would have one of my professors look it over to be sure it was good. For big scholarships that someone at my school had won in the past, I would ask the person who had won to look it over and compare it to the one they had written."

– Mackenzie Mylod, Student, Graduated Debt-Free

Basic essay requirements

Before we get started on the "what" to write, let's cover the "how" to write your essays.

 COURSE MEMBERS

We have replays of Essay Hot Seats where we reviewed essays under 'Bonuses' for you! There is also the Essay Hot Seat workbook, which has a printable checklist summarizing the most important points.

Most essays have a word or character requirement. In school, word requirements ensure you do not write too little; with scholarships, they are typically used so that you do not write too much. Do not, and I repeat, please do not exceed essay word requirements. If it says 250 words maximum, utilize the full 250 words but **do not exceed 250**. Your application can actually be thrown out if you do not follow the essay requirements.

The next point I would like to make is that you have to make sure your essays are **grammatically correct**. The biggest tip I can offer here is to always have at least one other person check it for you. When I applied for scholarships, I had multiple teachers and professors help me throughout the process, but there was one teacher who consistently went through every single one of my essays. There will inevitably be errors, even with auto-correct in Microsoft Word or Google Docs, so please get an extra pair of eyes to take a look.

A fun trick is to read the essay out loud. You'll often stumble over the words if there is an error, run-on sentence, missing comma, incorrect word, and more. It's a great proofreading technique prior to passing it on to your chosen proofreader!

Who can review your essays? I highly suggest reaching out to a teacher or professor. Not only are they experienced in writing essays, but it is also a great opportunity to get to know them better. You can also have family members and your accountability partners look at them. The challenge with family members is that being an adult doesn't necessarily mean they are qualified to review creative writing. There are specific strategies to implement in order to write creative, attention-grabbing essays. Typically an English teacher or professor would be better equipped unless your parent, guardian, or other adult in your life has a background in literature or creative writing. Lastly, at The Scholarship System, we offer essay reviews using our decade of reading thousands of essays. Whatever you choose, you want <u>at least</u> one other highly experienced person to read over them.

COURSE MEMBERS

You receive a discount for essay reviews. Please find "Essay Reviews" within your course portal.

Another great place to run your essay through is Grammarly. They have a free version that will check for basic errors. You can pay if you want it to check for more complicated issues with the essay. This does not replace the human you want to review your essay, but just like reading your essay out loud, this is a great pre-check you can do before handing it to someone so you don't waste their time.

Lastly, try to format your essays nicely. Some scholarships will just have you paste your essay into an online form, but keeping your essays double-spaced, size 12 font and Times New Roman, Arial, or another professional font while in Microsoft Word or any other tool you use will keep them clean in case you do need to print and mail them. Also, this makes it easier on the people reviewing your essays. If you have the space and the software allows, try to break up paragraphs to make it more reader-friendly. Just remember: appearance is important in this case!

The Scholarship System's 3-Step Writing Method

You may find this hard to believe, but I HATED writing. Yes, me, a 6-figure scholarship winner who had to write essays to earn that money and someone who ended up writing a book! I actually had a near-failing score in Literature one year but was lucky enough that my teacher allowed us to rewrite essays as many times as we wanted to bring up our score. As you can imagine, I spent a lot of time rewriting papers and essays for that class.

All that changed when I figured out our 3-step writing method. I used this to write this book, but I also used it in my personal life, writing blogs, brainstorming speeches, and so much more.

In fact, many of our course members have told us they now use this writing method to write their papers for school!

> *"For me, The Scholarship System's writing method was the big thing, especially the mind mapping. My brain is very scattered. I am an artistic, creative person so my thoughts kind of bounce around. Mind-mapping was like a great way to have organized chaos to keep that creativity without having an overly linear line of thought that persisted throughout the essay. That was huge for me. I now use it on my papers for school because it's so much more efficient."*

– Sydney, Won Over $50,000 in Scholarships

Why does The Scholarship System's Writing Method work?

First, it'll get you thinking creatively and outside of the box. No one wants to read a boring, dry essay that sounds like a research paper. Instead, we want it to be memorable so judges pick us as the winner!

Second, it helps get you going even if you're stuck or hate writing. These three steps you're about to learn help even those who hate writing like me because you don't have to sit down starting at a blank Word or Google Doc. Instead, you get to grab a sheet of paper and start doodling more or less. How much more fun is that?

Third, our writing method basically creates the entire essay before you even sit down in front of a document. Sitting in front of a document, your brain begins to think linearly. Again, that isn't what we want at first. We want creative. Then, when it comes time to write or type, you'll already have a structure that has creative aspects to it. You just need to fluff it up!

To sum it up, this method is a huge golden nugget and will help you not just on scholarship essays but any writing in your future. Let's dive in!

Step 1: Brainstorm Your Essay

Remember back in elementary school when a teacher taught you how to do 'spider webs' of ideas to help you form your essay? I am not sure about you, but I know I never actually listened to them—until now. The brainstorming 'spider web' that was taught to us years ago is actually called mind-mapping and helped me write this entire book. It actually works!

When you sit down to write an essay and start writing in sentences in a document, you are writing, and therefore thinking, linearly. However, if you use the mind-mapping approach, you force your mind to be more creative, therefore forming a more effective essay. If you want to write an award-winning essay, you have to be creative. Here is how to mind-map:

In the center of a blank sheet of paper, write the topic that you need to write about. For example, say the essay question is: Name a time that you had to overcome a difficult challenge. How did you overcome it? In the center of the paper, you can write "CHALLENGES" and then circle that word.

Then, stemming off that first word, simply keep writing any words or phrases that come to mind regarding the topic. Scatter these words all over the sheet of paper and connect them to what the idea stemmed from, typically the topic of the essay.

It's best to jot down examples or stories that show your point versus just telling them your point. What does that mean? Here's an example: Say the essay asked for a quality to help you succeed in college. I can simply write "I am organized," or I can paint a picture of being organized. Is there a time in my life where I took organization to another level? Did I neatly arrange all my parents' documents, photos, and folders in alphabetical order at a very young age, not realizing it was the start of my obsession with being organized? Try to think of stories you can add to make your points more memorable. You don't want to write the entire story down on the mind map. Just put a couple words that will remind you of the experience so you can refer to that later in Step 2 and Step 3 of our writing method. So with this example, I'd write "ORGANIZED," and then I'd create a separate bubble and write "organizing parents' documents" and then try to think of a few other examples.

If you find a piece of your mind map that you want to run with, feel free to start a new sheet of paper with that specific idea in the middle. Don't rush this part. This is the bulk of the work and will make your essay more memorable and easier to write!

Step 2: Outline Your Essay

Once you have a full sheet of random thoughts, you may find a topic or two that clearly have more ideas stemming off them than others. This is probably the route you want to take for writing your essay. The next step is to form an outline from them. Group the words or phrases into two or three main ideas and write this down as your outline. Within each point, you'll want to refer to the story you want to mention in your essay. Remember: SHOW, don't tell. You may find one point is enough for an entire essay. Or perhaps you end up taking multiple points and stories to formulate the essay. This is where you can be creative! Here is an example outline:

Parent lost job
- *budgeting*
- *no eating out*
- *part-time work to help*
- *stress on our family*
  - *story 1 - Family meeting to discuss situation*
  - *story 2 - Needed new shoes for cheer*

Overwhelmed with everything
- *job*
- *cheer practice on own because didn't make team*
- *sick pet*
- *had to learn time management*
  - *story 1 - crazy day, late to job and promised never again, had to make changes*
  - *story 2 - making schedule with parents*

How these will help me in college & beyond
- *money management*
- *time management*
- *stress management*
- *power of positivity*

Step 3: Write Your Essay

After you complete a quick outline, you are ready to start writing. It is amazing how quickly you can write a phenomenal essay using this method. When you sit down to finally start writing or typing, have your mind map and outline in front of you. At this point, it's just about filling in the gaps between your main points and crafting it as a story. Again, pay attention to word count! We'll talk more about reusing essays later but this is also a great example of where we could use perhaps one story from the essay for a shorter version and adapt it versus starting from scratch. Let's get into more detail on how to craft a great essay.

Selling Yourself in an Essay

Now that you have the ideas and an outline, let's talk about how to sell yourself in an essay.

The beginning of your essay should always grab the judges' attention. I always liked to start off with a quote or a story of some sort. When mind-mapping, I am sure some of your thoughts related to a story somehow. That would be a perfect way to begin. Either way, you never want to just start by rephrasing the essay question. That is very bland and probably half of your competitors are doing that. You want to start off with something that is mind-boggling or thought-provoking.

Here are a few examples:

 Essay question: In your opinion, what is the greatest challenge that your generation will face? What ideas do you have for dealing with this issue?

Sample response:

"As the years go on, every individual is becoming more and more independent as well as self-sufficient – especially women. While this is an advantage, I am afraid my generation will forget that together we must make a whole - whether it consists of all United States citizens, employees for a single company, or even members of one household. Individuals can only go so far on their own and, in order to truly succeed, everyone needs to work together for a brighter future. That said, I believe the greatest challenge my generation will face involves unification as a country, community or even family."

 Essay question: Describe yourself creatively.

"I am a sweet potato pie. Sweet potato pies are treasured for their comfort and beauty, but beneath their golden-brown crust and burnt orange filling, there is significantly more. By learning to bake a sweet potato pie, you will only begin to grasp the complexity of who I am.

First, boil the sweet potatoes...."

Hopefully you see what I mean after those examples. They began with a story or thought-provoking point. Some were extremely creative, too. Now the next step is the body of the essay.

You want to keep the body very structured. As I said earlier, try to form your thoughts into three main ideas. This will help you keep the essay organized and easy to follow. In addition to keeping it organized, try to keep them interested throughout the entire essay. There are many power words out there that help demonstrate how awesome you are. To make it even easier on you, I put a huge list at the back. These are the same words that are typically used in resumes because they are power words that catch anyone's attention. For example, of the two sentences below, which sounds better?

1. When I was part of the ACE club, I helped start a fundraiser that raised $1,000 for a charity.

2. **Establishing** a <u>successful</u> fundraiser with my team in the ACE Club, we **achieved our goal** of raising $1,000 for a charity.

The second sentence sounds much more impressive. Those keywords like 'establish' and 'achieve' are great buzz words. Try to spice up what you are saying with buzz words like these because not only do they catch attention, they also articulate what you are trying to say in a better way.

Lastly, do not undersell yourself. Overall, your goal is to show that experiences throughout your life make you qualified for the scholarship award. Earlier in the book we discussed many different scenarios that can be used in essays as selling points such as helping a neighbor, volunteering with a small organization, leading a shift at work, etc. Keep in mind that all of these are challenging experiences and therefore valid responses. If the essay asks you about a challenge, do not say, "Well, I have had a pretty easy life," because that does not do anything for you. You must develop something of substance that sells you.

Let's recap:

1. Start off with an interesting story, quote, or phrase that catches the reader's attention. Do NOT rephrase the question.

2. Structure the essay around three main points (as long as word count permits) so that it is organized and easy to follow.

3. Include popular power words to sell yourself.

4. Do not undersell yourself. Remember: you need the money, too!

4. Miscellaneous Scholarship Requirements

My goal is to prepare you so there are no surprises when you apply for scholarships. Here are the last few items that many scholarships ask for. Once again, not all will, but at least you are prepared.

FAFSA results – They will ask about your Student Aid Index (SAI), previously known as the Estimated Family Contribution (EFC) in some scholarship applications, so make sure you complete your FAFSA as we discussed at the beginning of the book.

Transcripts – Most committees require official, sealed transcripts from your guidance office but sometimes you can send in a printout or PDF from your school instead. If the scholarship accepts a printed copy or PDF for the application, they will often ask for an official transcript later if you are selected as a recipient.

SAT/ACT scores – Some scholarships simply ask for your scores and do not require any official documentation. Others may require your official scores from the College Board.

The SAT and ACT both allow you to send your scores for free to a certain number of recipients if you write them down at registration, but it will cost you a small amount after that. If you have free or reduced-cost lunch in school, you can get waivers for a lot of this so ask your counselor if that is available to you.

Resume – Few scholarships actually ask for a resume but I always suggest submitting or sending one if you can. Having a solid resume as a high school student can be impressive as long as you have it properly done. I submitted a resume with almost all of my applications because it gave them additional information that I may not have been able to fit in the application. One point to keep in mind, however, this is very similar to an essay and you should make sure it does not have any spelling errors, uses power words, grabs attention, sells your accomplishments, etc. It is not worth sending if it does not help you!

 COURSE MEMBERS
Please check out Step 5 for specific essay examples, worksheets, resume template, and more!

5. The 'Anything Else?' Essay

Many scholarships give you space to share any other information you feel is important. You should **always** take advantage of this opportunity. Remember when we talked about less-than-perfect test scores or grades? This is your chance to explain that. Did you really want to share your amazing experience leading a team to success in school? Here you go! Whatever you think will put the cherry on top of your application needs to be in this essay, so, once again, please do not skip this!

I could go on forever with suggestions for writing your essays, but this foundation is what you need to write some killer, award-winning essays. Just keep in mind that it takes practice. Working with the person who is reviewing your scholarship essays over and over again will only improve your writing skills and make your applications stronger each time. So do not just write a few essays and say, "Geeze, I did not win anything." Instead, keep writing them and improving them constantly and, with that, keep applying. The more applications you submit, the higher your chances are of winning!

Packaging – Putting Your Best Foot Forward Through Presentation

Remember the saying "Do not judge a book by its cover"? Unfortunately, this does not apply in the scholarship process. Judges will judge your application by its appearance. Why? Let's just think: If one judge gets two applications, both are of the same quality and have decent essays but one was nicely formatted, printed on clean sheets of paper, stapled together in the order the application requested and the other is just a ton of loose-leaf sheets of paper in no order with grammatical errors, which one do you think they will select? The orderly one!

This applies to online submissions as well. Uploading documents where the formatting gets messed up, has errors, is not named clearly to label requirements, etc., can all make the judges' lives harder and, therefore, decrease your chances of winning.

So how can you make sure your application is not thrown away for silly reasons?

First, I highly suggest putting your essays and all other requirements in the order they were listed on the application. Secondly, and I know I already said this but it is worth repeating, ensure there are no spelling or other grammatical errors anywhere. Lastly, put all of these in one nice, neat envelope for delivery if a physical application or put them all into one clean, orderly PDF file if uploading documents. If pasting into forms, ensure your paste format didn't mess things up.

If you are submitting online, which many scholarships have moved to, your life is simpler; however, please make sure all sections are filled out correctly and, if you can, format your essays nicely after pasting them such as putting spaces between paragraphs and indenting paragraphs.

Recap

I suggest scanning through this chapter each time you are about to submit an application to make sure you did not forget anything. Also, do not forget about all the resources at the back of the book as well as on our website: **www.thescholarshipsystem.com**. The more time you spend up front finding the right scholarships and working on your essays and perfecting them, the less time you will spend down the road because you will be able to reuse them just like I did. More on this soon.

Between the research skills you have developed and the writing suggestions we covered, you are a scholarship guru right now. In the final chapter, we are going to cover basic logistics of how to handle your newly found cash but also, more importantly, how to turn this into a repeatable system; hence, The Scholarship System. Creating a well-oiled machine with your scholarship process is how you can really bring in the money because, like I've said many times, this is not a one-time application and you magically have a free ride. Or at least that is not the case for most students. But it also doesn't have to take endless numbers of hours either. We have learned many tips and tricks over the years on how to simplify this process and streamline it so you can save time and focus on what matters: submitting applications. Let's go!

Artificial Intelligence (AI) and Scholarships

The world of Artificial Intelligence (AI) is changing rapidly. By the time I finish typing this chapter, things will probably have already changed. That said, there's no denying the disruption this technology is making to so many industries. Scholarships are not excluded from that. Whether good or not, it is our new reality so I want to cover some of the ways we can use it as well as ways we absolutely should not.

First, if you aren't familiar with AI, you can quickly Google it and find millions of results. AI has consumed information from the web, books, podcasts, etc., and has 'learned' from them. It has the ability to answer questions for you, summarize meetings, generate fake images, write papers, create presentations, edit videos, and so much more.

The challenge with AI is there are very few rules around it as of right now. That doesn't mean it's a free-for-all. Abusing AI can hurt you if done incorrectly.

The most important point I want to make here is that you never want to ask AI to write an essay or complete an application for you. Yes, it technically can; however, the quality typically won't be that high and certainly not creative or personal. AI doesn't know you like you do. It can't add emotion and touch the judges' hearts like you can. Additionally, and most importantly, scholarship committees are running essays through AI-checkers and disqualifying anyone who used AI to write their responses. In fact, in The Scholarship System, we did this and will continue to do so when choosing our annual scholarship winners.

Recently, college graduates had their diplomas withdrawn because they were accused of letting AI write their final papers. Professors and teachers are using AI checkers as well. Please do not cheat using these tools.

If we can't have AI write our essays or do our applications for us, how can we use AI? Here are a few quick ideas.

First, you can ask one of the AI platforms for a list of scholarships. Like we taught in Step 3, be specific. For example, you can ask for "a list of 20 scholarship applications due in April for women in science." This has its limitations. When I ran these searches out of curiosity, it couldn't find a full 20 so it just repeated the same list after it ran out of results versus saying it could only find 11. If I wasn't paying attention, I would've thought I had twice the number of scholarships I truly had. That said, the initial 11 were at least a start and I could use my discernment skills from Step 3 to narrow those down to ones I am actually eligible for.

Second, you can ask AI for power words or buzz words around a specific scenario in your life. You can also ask it for ideas for topics. These are perhaps pushing the limit, but I think they're okay as long as you are still writing the essay yourself.

Third, you can ask it to proofread your essay. You may also be able to put your essay into the AI platform and ask it to shorten it to so many words if it is over the targeted word count. Again, this is probably not going to result in the best version, but it may give you ideas on how to shorten sentences.

As new technology develops, things will constantly and rapidly change. Overall, we say use it very sparsely throughout your scholarship journey.

Creating a Scholarship System

Closing The Deal So More Money Comes Your Way

In this book, we have covered a lot of material. If you have made it to this point, you are a scholarship-applying machine ready to win some money for college. I honestly am so excited for you!

We covered the basic financial aid 101 so that you understand all the different options you have. We then calculated how much school will cost you if you take out a loan, which was not too pretty, I am sure. Hopefully that gave you some serious motivation to complete this book; however, we also went over getting in the money-making mindset, which is one of the most important steps in The Scholarship System because if you do not feel motivated to go through this process, you will not see the results you want.

After getting you in the mindset with some goal setting, we then covered where to find scholarships and cash awards. You should have already found at least five scholarships that specifically match your characteristics so that you do not waste any time on scholarships that do not pertain to you.

Next, we went through a ton of different worksheets to help you find your competitive qualities and discover how you can sell them. Once we figured out what you can talk about on your applications, we covered how to apply, including the basic requirements of applications, how to write a killer essay in no time that you can reuse, and all the miscellaneous requirements you may see. The last step we covered was how to package your application so that it is presentable, professional, and award-winning.

Now that is a lot of information! BUT—we are not finished yet.

Let's talk about handling this money and then turning your process into a well-oiled system so that you keep bringing in more each year.

Receiving Your Big Bucks

Once you learn you are the winner and have to receive scholarship money (yes, I am that confident in you! It's going to happen!), you will most likely have to send in your school's information so that they can send the money to the university. This will be how most scholarships are handled, though it can vary. We've had some families receive their winnings as a Visa gift card! And don't forget cash awards for students already in college. Those are typically cash checks sent directly to the student right after they're selected (of course, these are our favorite).

"Have worked hard on finding small local scholarships, thanks to your advice! Have one from the chamber of commerce for a college fair they hosted! $500 Visa card!"

– Cheryl, Student's Mother, Ended With a Free Ride
Plus $250 Overage Check

If your university caps the amount you can receive and you meet that amount, you can request the check to be sent directly to you. I do not suggest doing this until your entire bill is paid for! Otherwise, you risk spending it on non-necessity items. If your bill does not use up all the funding, the university will actually cut you a check for the remaining amount. This is called an overage check, which I received every single semester while in college. It is beautiful, I promise.

Thank You Letters

Someone put this money toward a scholarship so that they can help students like you; therefore, it is a nice gesture to thank them when you get it. It does not have to be anything incredible, but a simple thank you card can go a long way.

In the resources section, I created an outline for a solid thank you note. I suggest getting blank thank you cards or handwriting a letter. If your handwriting is truly illegible, you can type the thank you letter, but it will not seem nearly as personal as you writing it yourself. Another opportunity to thank them is when you graduate. No matter the occasion, let them know what you majored in, your future plans, and how their scholarship helped you get there. It is so rewarding to hear you made an impact on someone else's life. Let them hear it!

Tax Implications

When I received my scholarship money, I was worried that I would have to pay taxes on it. By my senior year, I had thousands of dollars that were over my university bill so I was especially worried. I have good news for you—you do not have to pay taxes on your scholarship money as long as it is proven to be used for college bills. Now I am no accountant and laws change all the time, so always speak to a CPA or your guardians' tax representative, but here are the basic rules I learned to play by:

Scholarships are tax-free when used for:

1. Tuition and fees to enroll in an accredited institution
2. Fees, books, supplies and equipment required for your courses
- Please note: This is anything "required" for your courses which means, if you can prove it was required, you have a little wiggle room here. Remember to keep receipts for any expenses paid for college outside of your typical tuition bill paid through your university. There are tax credits for expenses as well, though that's beyond the range of this book. Again, speak to your CPA (or your parents'/guardians' CPA) and they should be able to help you here!

Scholarship money is taxable when used for:

1. Room and board
2. Travel
3. Research

You will receive a tax sheet, the 1098-T form, each year from your university regardless of whether or not it is taxable. It will detail the total bill your university charged, including all expenses paid, and any scholarship funds you received. If you had an excess amount of scholarships over your college bill, you (the student) have to report this in your taxes for the past year. Cash awards or any scholarships sent directly to you should provide a 1099 form so you are still tax compliant since they won't be reported through your school.

This did not impact my parents in any way. For more information, I suggest looking on the IRS website and speaking with a CPA. I always had a part-time job, which I believe evened out any potential tax bill for my overages. Still, if you're facing this and trying to figure it out, it means you should have a free ride, which is a pretty nice situation to be in!

Creating Your Own Scholarship System

Anastasiya put the scholarship process into words perfectly:

"Searching for scholarships could be very rewarding, but it could also be very time consuming. Plan to dedicate several hours a week to this. The more scholarships you apply to, the higher are your chances of receiving the financial aid you're searching for."

While I know this sounds like a lot of work, you can put strategies into place to make your life easier and save you time. In fact, if you've been implementing this book as you read, you've already created some of those materials! The goal is to create reusable materials or reference materials so that you not only save time but also avoid missing things or making mistakes.

When deciding where to put these materials, I still highly recommend some sort of cloud-based system such as Google Drive or Dropbox. Saving them on your computer or printing them out can be risky. I am speaking from experience. I dropped my laptop freshman year in college and lost everything. Unfortunately, I didn't sync everything to an online platform. I was able to find many of my materials in my emails but many weren't the final versions. I was devastated! Please don't make my mistake.

Another time the cloud-based system saved me was when I once realized I had a deadline that day but wasn't anywhere near my laptop. I simply logged into my Dropbox from the library computer and was able to access my essay, submitting it on time.

Here is a list of materials you can put together to use for future applications:

1. **Activities and Awards Document** – Update each year or semester, including throughout college.
2. **Essays** – Save multiple versions of these versus saving over the same one each time. Save all the different variations if you're reusing an essay for different word counts, labeling the essay with the word count.
3. **Transcripts** – Any PDF versions
4. **Recommendation Letters** if the recommender is comfortable sending you a copy.
5. **Resume**
6. **Any other materials** you have had to submit. You never know when you can use them again!

By collecting these materials and saving them in one **cloud-based** location, you may be able to reuse them and knock out an entire application in under an hour!

"Once she had done a number of different essays, it got a lot easier because she could simply cut and paste. With the money she has received with your program, she will be able to attend the private school of her choice and will be able to spend less time working and more time volunteering and engaging in other campus activities. She will graduate debt-free!"

– Kalene, Mother of Student Who Won Over $92,500

Reusing Essays

When reusing essays, it is critical you have the new versions reviewed again. It can be very easy to make mistakes when your eyes are familiar with text, such as an essay you've spent hours poring over. Essays can be reused when prompts are the same but word counts vary or where a common story in your life can be used to answer multiple prompts. For example, perhaps you've had a health condition you've faced your entire life. A story about this may be able to answer a prompt about challenges you've faced, characteristics that will help you succeed in college and beyond, what you want to be in the future, and more! This is where you can really begin to save time. When you crack that story that really sells the judges, you can often use it over and over again. In fact, that's exactly what I did. My winning essay was used for multiple years of applying for scholarships!

Lastly, when reusing essays, it's important that you aren't submitting the same essay over and over if you are NOT winning. In that case, you'll just keep getting the same result. You only want to reuse proven, winning essays!

If you need help tweaking an essay to improve your chances, go back to the review section under Step 5 and decide who is the next best person to help you with your essays!

 COURSE MEMBERS

You have videos explaining how to reuse essays, going over specific examples inside Step 5 under the essay lessons!

Conclusion

I am honored to have been able to share all this experience with you. Over the course of a decade, I have seen thousands of applications, essays, and students going through the scholarship process. There is a lot that this process entails but I am completely confident that you can do it.

Otherwise, you would not have made it to the end of the book. I hope you enjoyed The Scholarship System and all the tools and worksheets we went through. I am so excited for you to start winning your scholarship award money right away.

Remember: Do not stop once you graduate high school! If you can master this process and continue doing it until your senior year in college, you can make more and more money each year. Perhaps you can even get enough to pay off any loan balances from the first year if need be. Just keep applying for as many scholarships as possible as long as you truly meet the criteria.

If you think you would work better with videos, worksheets, and support, you may want to consider our online course, The Scholarship System. You can learn more at **www.thescholarshipsystem.com/info**. You can also follow us on social media for more tips and tricks on not only the scholarship process but all things paying for college.

Overall, we've created an organization built to help you secure scholarships and minimize the student loan debt you have to borrow. These strategies not only worked for me but for thousands of families across the nation. And they can work for you, too! It's just a matter of implementing. Don't put this book down and say you'll come back later and implement the steps. Start NOW!

I wish you the best of luck! Now go make some money!

Free Resources

We created a webpage for you listing
all the amazing resources we've mentioned
in this book!

Visit the link below to begin using
these free tools.

www.thescholarshipsystem.com/
action-guide

Enjoying the book?

Consider leaving your feedback!

I greatly appreciate you taking the time to read The Scholarship System. As a self-publisher, it means the world to me and hope it makes a huge difference in your journey of paying for college.

If you have 60 seconds to spare, it would help me tremendously if you could leave a short review on Amazon. It does wonders with helping the book reach more families in need and I love hearing how you benefited from it.

To leave your feedback:

Open your camera app.
Point the device at the QR code below and
click the yellow visit button.
The review page will open for you to submit!

OR visit **www.thescholarshipsystem.com/bookreview**
or find us on Amazon by simply searching
"The Scholarship System."

The Scholarship System Resources

ACCOUNTABILITY PARTNER LIST

Name	Goal to Help With	Meeting Frequency	Method for Meeting
Ex. John Smith	Completing 5 scholarship applications by winter break	Every Wednesday at 8:00PM	Google Hangout or Zoom

PASSWORD PROTECTOR

It is very easy to lose passwords, whether they are for sites to find scholarships or even sites where you are applying. Use this table to keep track of all the usernames and passwords you need. This should keep you from having to search everywhere for your information every time you start your research or applications. Please remember, you can also use The Scholarship System's free app and Chrome Extension to document information, passwords, URLs, and so much more as you find scholarships. Learn more at **www.thescholarshipsystem.com/app**.

Site	Username	Password

SCHOLARSHIP TRACKER

Scholarship 1 Requirements

Scholarship 1
Site:

Login Info:

Due date:

Scholarship 2 Requirements

Scholarship 2
Site:

Login Info:

Due date:

Scholarship 3 Requirements

Scholarship 3
Site:

Login Info:

Due date:

_____
_____
_____
_____
_____

Scholarship 4 Requirements

Scholarship 4
Site:

Login Info:

Due date:

_____
_____
_____
_____
_____

Scholarship 5 Requirements

Scholarship 5
Site:

Login Info:

Due date:

_____
_____
_____
_____
_____

Scholarship 6 Requestments

Scholarship 6
Site:

Login Info:

Due date:

_____
_____
_____
_____
_____

Six scholarship applications are not enough to get a free ride. Make copies of the Scholarship Tracker sheets and keep applying!

THANK YOU NOTE OUTLINE

Dear _____,
I wanted to thank you for the __(scholarship name here)__ scholarship. Without it, I would not be able to __(what would happen if you didn't receive funding?)__. I am now majoring in __ (major here)__ which I plan to use as a (profession you plan to go into). I also am getting involved in (organizations, clubs, activities you have joined).

Overall, my college experience is (adjective here such as great, amazing, life-changing) and you are part of the reason I am here. So once again, thank you for (contributing/creating/donating) to the (scholarship name here) scholarship. You have helped me get one step closer to my future success.

Best regards,

(Your name & contact information)

Power Words for Essays

Able	Earned	Managed	Recommended
Accomplished	Educated	Marketed	Redesigned
Achievement	Encourage	Maximized	Reengineered
Action	Enhance	Mediated	Represented
Advanced	Enhanced	Mentored	Restructured
Analysis	Established	Modernized	Retained
Analyzed	Evaluate	Motivated	Revised
Assist	Evaluated	Negotiated	Revitalized
Audited	Examined	Nourished	Safeguarded
Built	Facilitate	Observed	Secured
Closed	Facilitated	Obtained	Selected
Collaborated	Forecasted	Operated	Spearheaded
Committed	Formulate	Organized	Specified
Conduct	Fulfilled	Originated	Standardized
Conducted	Gained	Overhauled	Strengthened
Consult	Gathered	Oversaw	Structured
Contributed	Gave	Participated	Suggested
Coordinated	Generated	Performed	Superseded
Counseled	Headed	Pioneered	Supervised
Defined	Hosted	Planned	Targeted
Delegated	Identified	Prepared	Taught
Deliver	Impacted	Presented	Tested
Delivered	Implemented	Processed	Trained
Demonstrated	Improved	Promoted	Transcended
Design	Improvised	Prospected	Tutored
Develop	Increased	Provided	Unified
Developed	Influenced	Published	Upgraded
Devoted	Justified	Pursued	Utilized
Distinguished	Launched	Quantified	Validated
Diversified	Lobbied	Ranked	Valued
Drove	Maintained	Received	Wrote

Mind Map Example

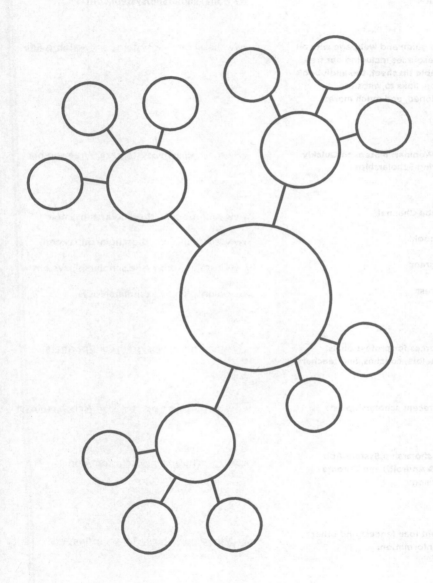

The Scholarship System
Free Resources Summary

Website:	**www.thescholarshipsystem.com**
Audio guide and webpage with all free resources including our free printable tip sheet, the audiobook version, links to websites mentioned, and much more:	www.thescholarshipsystem.com/**action-guide**
Free Webinar: 6 Steps to Quickly Securing Scholarships	www.thescholarshipsystem.com/**freewebinar**
Youtube Channel:	www.youtube.com/**thescholarshipsystem**
Facebook:	www.facebook.com/**thescholarshipsystem**
Instagram:	www.instagram.com/**the.scholarshipsystem**
Pinterest:	www.pinterest.com/**scholarshipsys**
Resources for professionals, counselors, coaches, and teachers:	www.thescholarshipsystem.com/**partners**
Most recent scholarship list:	www.thescholarshipsystem.com/**scholarshiplist**
The Scholarship System App (iOS & Android) and Chrome Extension:	www.thescholarshipsystem.com/**app**
Student loan lenders and other loan information:	www.thescholarshipsystem.com/**lenders**

Made in United States
Troutdale, OR
11/15/2024

24862130R00080